Vitamins

A full explanation of these thr......................... and
how to balance them in the diet or from supplements to
maintain and improve your health.

VITAMINS ADK
All You Need to know to Ensure a Balanced Intake

by

Leonard Mervyn
B.Sc., Ph.D., F.R.S.C.

THORSONS PUBLISHERS LIMITED
Wellingborough, Northamptonshire

First published 1984

© LEONARD MERVYN 1984

British Library Cataloguing in Publication Data

Mervyn, Leonard,
  Vitamins ADK
  1. Vitamins   2. Vitamins in human condition
  I. Title
  613.2'8   QP771

  ISBN 0-7225-0872-7

Printed in Great Britain by
Richard Clay (The Chaucer Press) Ltd,
Bungay, Suffolk

CONTENTS

INTRODUCTION

The three vitamins, A, D and K, whilst apparently unrelated in their functions and metabolism, do exhibit some common properties. All are fat-soluble, which means that their absorption from the diet is dependent upon the same sort of mechanisms that exist for fats and oils. When these mechanisms break down, as in certain diseases and hereditary conditions, the malabsorption of these vitamins can lead to deficiency.

Each of the vitamins is available from two distinct sources and it is likely that, under ideal circumstances, one source of each vitamin would suffice to prevent deficiency. Hence, whilst vitamin A as such is available only from animal, fish and poultry-derived foods, its precursor beta-carotene is widely distributed in plant foods and is quite capable of supplying all the individual's needs. Vitamin D is poorly distributed in natural foods, and only then in those of animal origin. Yet when the body is given an adequate exposure to sunshine, all its requirements can be met from this source. This mechanism is independent of absorption from the intestine, so it represents the only way a person suffering from fat malabsorption problems can get their vitamin D.

Vitamin K, too, can be supplied, probably in adequate quantity, by the bacteria that inhabit the large intestine, but at the same time Nature has provided it in many foods. Therefore, when absorption of fats is normal, there is little likelihood of anyone developing vitamin K deficiency although, as we shall see, certain medicinal drugs can play a part in preventing the utilization of that vitamin.

Despite the fact that vitamins A and D are usually regarded as being provided together, at least in fish liver oils and liver, their functions appeared to be completely unrelated. Recent studies, however, suggest that vitamin A may have a part to play in the maintenance of healthy bones, so it may complement the function of vitamin D in that tissue. Both vitamins also share the common property of not acting within the body in the form in which they are absorbed from the food. Vitamin D is completely inactive until the liver and kidney convert it to 1,25 dihydroxy D which is the functioning form. Vitamin A, provided as retinol or beta-carotene, must be oxidized to the aldehyde or acid form before it can function in maintaining healthy sight and skin respectively. We know little about the metabolic form of vitamin K but it appears to be that in which it is provided, produced and absorbed.

Vitamin A has the dubious distinction of having the highest incidence of deficiency in the world as a whole, according to WHO sources. In certain areas it is closely followed by vitamin D despite this vitamin's potential source from the action of sunshine on skin. Deficiency of vitamin K is not confined to any particular global areas and is usually the result of malabsorption of fats or prolonged use of antibiotics rather than reduced dietary intake.

All three vitamins are toxic when taken in excessive amounts and for this reason they are controlled by legislation in the potencies that can be offered for general sale to the public. The symptoms of overdose of vitamin A and D are well documented and they are discussed in detail under their respective headings. Vitamin K overdose is fairly rare and has never been associated with dietary intake, but is usually the result of medical treatment to overcome excessive use of anticoagulant drugs.

There are few cases on record, but we may assume that one result of excess vitamin K is an increased tendency to form blood clots. It must be stated however that evidence of this actually happening is very sparse. The reason is that vitamin K is not a blood clotting factor in its own right but functions via four protein factions that set the coagulation process in motion. Until the effects of excess vitamin K are known clearly however it is best to rely upon good dietary sources of the vitamin and leave supplementation to those best able to monitor its effects.

1.

A – THE VISION VITAMIN

Discovery

The first demonstration of an accessory food factor, later known as vitamin A, is attributed to the British biochemist Sir Frederick Gowland Hopkins. Between 1906 and 1912 he showed that a diet composed of the only known food factors at that time, namely casein (protein), starch and sugar (carbohydrates), lard (fat) and inorganic mineral salts, was insufficient to maintain young rats and mice in health, with the result that they failed to thrive and eventually died. Incorporating small amounts of milk into this diet increased its nutritional value tremendously and the young rodents grew normally and remained healthy. It was reasoned therefore that milk contained some factor or factors that were needed to supply the complete diet.

Within the next two years this factor was shown to be fat-soluble by simply extracting milk with ether – a fat solvent. By means of the rat test the extracted milk was proved to be inactive when added to the purified diet, but the fat extracted by the ether prevented the symptoms induced by this same diet. Similar studies by two groups of workers enabled the accessory food factor to be isolated from butter (T.B. Osborne and L.B. Mendel) and from butter, egg-yolk and cod liver oil (E.V. McCollum and M. Davis). In 1915, the latter researchers proposed the name for the new factor to be 'fat-soluble A' to distinguish it from the 'water-soluble B' factor that they had already extracted from whey, yeast and rice polishings. Eventually the new factor was designated vitamin A. In 1918, E. Mellanby reported in *The Journal of Physiology* that the new factor A did not cure rickets, and so it was proved to be different from the 'fat-soluble D' factor that he had already demonstrated in cod liver oil.

Vitamin A is found only in food derived from animal sources although it can be made readily from a precursor that occurs specifically in lemon grass oil. However, although plant foods do not contain the vitamin as such, they supply colouring pigments called carotenoids, some of which are converted to vitamin A within the body. The most potent carotenoid is called beta-carotene and the relationship of this to vitamin A was first demonstrated in 1920 by O. Rosenheim and J. C. Drummond. They reported in *Lancet* that the potency of vegetable foods in replacing vitamin A was closely related to their content of carotene. This coloured pigment had been isolated from carrots almost a century before. Eventually, T. Moore at Cambridge University proved unequivocally that carotene gives rise to vitamin A but to this day the exact mechanism of the conversion is not known with certainty.

Nomenclature of Vitamin A

Vitamin A, in terms of its chemical structure, is a long-chain poly-unsaturated alcohol with a ring structure, called beta-ionone, at the opposite end of the chain to the hydroxyl (or alcohol) group. The names of all alcohol substances end in -ol, and so the approved name for vitamin A, is retinol.

Structure of Retinol

The originally isolated vitamin was initially called vitamin A1 and is known as the all-trans form of retinol. In terms of activity within the body it is the most potent form of the vitamin.

Fortunately, this is also the commonest form that

occurs in foods of animal origin. However, other types of retinol with slight geometrical changes in the polyunsaturated part of the molecule also occur in foods. These are known as isomers. One example is cis-vitamin A, or cis-retinol, but this has somewhat lower biological activity than the all-trans variety. Another example is vitamin A2, which is a naturally occurring slightly modified retinol, that is present in some fish livers but possesses only half the biological potency of retinol itself.

In the remainder of this book we shall use retinol and vitamin A as synonymous names for the all-trans form that is also the most active within the body. However, retinol occurs in foodstuffs in forms that are combined (or esterified) with fatty acids such as acetic or palmitic. The vitamin is then called retinyl acetate or retinyl palmitate. In these forms, vitamin A is often incorporated into tablets and capsules. These esters, however, possess full vitamin activity and are more stable than the uncombined retinol.

Hence retinol or retinyl esters occur as such in the food we eat but the body converts them to other, active forms of the vitamin. These are called retinal (short for retinaldehyde) and retinoic acid, both produced by oxidation of the alcohol end group of retinol. Later we shall see how important these oxidation products are in the metabolism of vitamin A.

The Relationship Between Vitamin A and Carotenoids

Carotenoids occur everywhere in the plant and animal kingdom, but those found in animals, mainly crustaceans (lobster, crabs etc.) and fish do not concern us here because they are not vitamin A precursors. However, it is interesting to note that, as colouring pigments, carotenoids play an essential role in their natural camouflage. In its natural environment the lobster is brown in colour, but when boiled the complex pigments break down to yield a bright red carotenoid that gives the lobster its characteristic colour. More than 100 carotenoids have now been isolated and characterized from natural sources. They are

responsible for most of the yellow-red colour of some
vegetables and fruits. The colourful changes that occur in
trees, shrubs and other plants during autumn are all due
to natural transformations of carotenoids. As far as
vitamin A is concerned, however, the most important
carotenoid is beta-carotene. This has a widespread distribution, usually in association with chlorophyll, the green
pigment of plants. In its chemical structure beta-carotene
can be regarded as two retinol molecules joined together
at the ends of the long chains. Hence it consists of two
beta-ionone rings, each at the end of a long polyunsaturated
carbon chain. It is the presence of a beta-ionone ring in a
carotenoid that confers upon it vitamin A precursor
activity. Beta-carotene contains two of these rings, so it is
the most potent pro-vitamin A. Some other carotenoids
contain only one beta-ionone ring, and amongst these are
alpha-carotene, gamma-carotene, cryptoxanthin and
beta-zeacarotene. These can also give rise to vitamin A
but at only half the level of beta-carotene. One of the
most widely distributed carotenoids, also associated with
chlorophyll, is called xanthophyll, but it is completely
devoid of vitamin A activity. The red pigment of tomatoes,
known as lycopene, also cannot be converted to retinol.

In addition to carrots, which are probably the richest
source of beta-carotene, dark green leaves also provide
useful amounts of this pro-vitamin A. In these, the yellow
colour of the carotene is masked by the stronger green of
chlorophyll. Red palm oil is rich in alpha-carotene, so it
too can provide significant quantities of vitamin A. It has
been calculated that in Europe and the United States of
America half of our daily intake of vitamin A comes from
the beta-carotene in the diet. However, where foods of
animal origin are not eaten by design, as in vegans and
some vegetarians, or by force of circumstance, as in the
poorer countries of the third world, all vitamin A requirements can be met from vegetable foods.

Quantitative Relationships
The conversion of beta-carotene to retinol takes place

mainly in the cells of the intestines in animals and man, but the liver is also a significant site where this happens. It would seem logical to expect beta-carotene, which we have seen is essentially two retinols stuck together, to split neatly down the middle of the long chain and so provide two molecules of the vitamin. Unfortunately this does not happen, and it is more likely that the beta-carotene is chewed up or oxidized at one end to yield only one molecule of vitamin A. This process, taken with the fact that beta-carotene is not very well absorbed from the food, means that 6 micrograms of it is equivalent to only 1 microgram of retinol in terms of biological activity. This relationship has been confirmed in many studies and is now widely accepted.

Beta-carotene became available in a pure form long before vitamin A, so it was reasonable to express the vitamin in international units (i.u.) and relate them to the pure carotene. Thus one i.u. of vitamin A was defined as equivalent to 0.6 micrograms of beta-carotene. Once vitamin A was obtained in a pure crystalline form it could be expressed in terms of microgram weight, so there was no longer a need for the arbitrary international units. Since 1969, all vitamin A activity has been expressed as retinol equivalents. It is worked out in diets by adding the retinol content to one-sixth of the beta-carotene content to give retinol equivalents in micrograms.

The relationships are as follows:

1 retinol equivalent = 1 microgram retinol
       = 6 micrograms beta-carotene
       = 12 micrograms other provitamin A carotenoids
       = 3.33 i.u. vitamin A activity from retinol
       = 10 i.u. vitamin A activity from beta-carotene

For the general public, vitamin A activity still tends to be associated with a certain number of i.u. but UK legislation now demands that it must be given as micrograms weight.

Thus, many supplements and foods express vitamin A content as micrograms but show the potency in i.u.'s as well using the conversion factor, 1 microgram = 3.33 i.u.

Dietary Sources of Retinol and Beta-carotene

Rich natural sources of pre-formed vitamin A (retinol) are dairy products, animal livers and kidneys, and the flesh of some fatty fish such as herring, salmon and mackerel. The liver oils of white fish, particularly cod, halibut and shark, represent the richest sources of the vitamin but these oils tend to be used more as a dietary supplement than as food items. The flesh of white fish supply only trace amounts of both vitamin A and carotene.

In addition to being useful sources of the vitamin itself, dairy products also provide reasonable quantities of beta-carotene. Similarly calf, lamb and ox livers contain beta-carotene, but in amounts that are small compared with the pre-formed vitamin A present. Both pig and chicken livers are devoid of carotene despite being rich sources of the vitamin. These differences in liver content presumably reflect varying dietary intake amongst the species, or possibly the pig and chicken are very efficient converters of carotene to vitamin A. Beef, lamb, pork and chicken meats, however, supply only traces of vitamin A and carotene.

Eggs are useful providers of pre-formed vitamin A with traces of carotene, but both substances are confined to the yolk. Egg white contains none of the vitamin nor its precursor. Margarine has no inherent vitamin A present but in most countries it is added by law, usually as beta-carotene, in amounts to make the potency equivalent to that in butter.

Many vegetables contain carotene but in varied concentrations. In green vegetables, the green outer leaves are good sources of carotene but the inner white leaves contain little. Carrots are probably the best natural source of beta-carotene but parsley comes close. Mushrooms, onions, turnips, potatoes, horseradish, cucumber, chicory, beetroot, celery, butter beans and haricot beans are completely or virtually devoid of carotenes, so they can be disregarded as sources of vitamin A.

The quantities of retinol and beta-carotene present in food items are given in Table 1.

Table 1

The Vitamin A and Carotene Contents of Foods

FOOD	VITAMIN A mcg/100g	CAROTENE mcg/100g
Cow's milk	35	22
Goat's milk	40	0
Butter	750	470
Cream – single	200	125
Cheese – hard	310	205
Cheese – cream	385	220
Cheese – cottage	32	18
Yogurt	8	5
Eggs – whole	140	Trace
Margarine – all kinds	900	0 (Unless fortified with carotene)
Liver – calf	14,600	100
– chicken	9,300	0
– lamb	18,100	60
– ox	16,500	1,540
– pig	9,200	0
Cod liver oil	18,000	Trace
Eel	1,200	Trace
Herring	45	Trace
Mackerel	45	Trace
Canned salmon	90	Trace
Asparagus	0	500
Beans – French	0	400
– Runner	0	400
– Broad	0	250
– Mung	0	24
Broccoli	0	2,500
Brussel sprouts	0	400
Cabbage – Savoy	0	300
– Spring	0	500
– Winter	0	300
Carrots	0	12,000

VITAMINS ADK

Table 1 (contd.)

FOOD	VITAMIN A mcg/100g	CAROTENE mcg/100g
Endives	0	2,000
Lettuce	0	1,000
Parsley	0	7,000
Peas	0	300
Peppers	0	200
Pumpkin	0	1,500
Spinach	0	6,000
Spring greens	0	4,000
Sweet potatoes	0	4,000
Tomatoes	0	600
Turnip tops	0	6,000
Watercress	0	3,000
Apricots	0	1,500
Bananas	0	200
Blackberries	0	100
Cherries	0	120
Blackcurrants	0	200
Redcurrants	0	70
Melons – Cantaloupe	0	2,000
– Yellow	0	100
Olives – green	0	180
– black	0	40
Peaches	0	500
Plums	0	220
Prunes	0	1,000
Tangerines	0	100
Orange Juice	0	50
Tomato juice	0	500

The Stability of Vitamin A and Carotene

Neither retinol nor the carotenes are soluble in water, so they do not suffer any losses by extraction into processing and cooking water. When they are present as pure oils, both vitamin A and beta-carotene are easily oxidized and hence lose activity. In the diet, however, they dissolve in the fats of the foods and are thus protected by natural anti-oxidants like vitamin E. Destruction of retinol and carotenes is increased by high temperatures and oxygen and is further accelerated by traces of the minerals and copper, although anti-oxidants do confer protection.

Considerable losses of vitamin A may occur in fish liver oils that are exposed to light for long periods, for example during display. In the absence of light and oxygen, carotene is remarkably stable. Dr Jack Drummond found that cooked carrots that had been sealed in air-tight containers in 1824, demonstrated much the same carotene content as fresh carrots when they were opened in 1939. Domestic cooking methods give rise to destruction rather than loss of vitamin A. Boiling water, for example, destroys 16% of the vitamin in margarine in 30 minutes; 20% in 1 hour and 40% in 2 hours.

Frying is more destructive – 40% is lost in 5 minutes; 60% in 10 minutes and 70% in 15 minutes. During the braising of liver, losses of the vitamin usually do not exceed 10%.

Freezing or canning, and subsequent cooking, of green vegetables containing mainly beta-carotene caused losses of 15-20% of their vitamin A activity; yellow vegetables containing mainly alpha-carotene lose between 30 and 35% by these cooking techniques. There is no difference in losses, despite varying temperatures and cooking times, between commercial canning, pressure cooking and conventional cooking methods.

The air-drying of vegetables and fruits can cause losses as low as 10-20% under controlled and mild commercial conditions. Traditional drying in the sun, on the other hand, causes virtual complete destruction of vitamin A activity.

Both retinol and carotene can be stabilized by absorbing them onto a starch-coated matrix of gelatin and sucrose in the presence of vitamin E as anti-oxidant. The resulting microbeads are widely used to supplement human and animal foods with vitamin A activity.

Our Requirements of Vitamin A
The daily requirements of vitamin A are shown in Table 2 (page 20). These must be regarded as the minimum needed to prevent deficiency but there is no real evidence that they are sufficient to maintain optimal health. Lower

values may suffice if all is presented as pre-formed vitamin A and higher values may be necessary if the diet suplies only beta-carotene.

Table 2

Recommended Daily Intakes of Vitamin A for the U.K.

Age Range (years)	Vitamin A (micrograms retinol equivalents)
0-1	450
1-7	300
7-9	400
9-12	575
12-15	725
15-18	750
18-75 plus	750
Pregnancy	750
Lactation	1,200

Absorption and Storage of Vitamin A

When eaten in the diet, vitamin A and beta-carotene are first emulsified to tiny globules in the intestine, like all fats and oils. The esters of vitamin A are split by digestive enzymes into the free alcohol form we call retinol. Absorption then takes place with the aid of emulsifying agents like bile. Within the cells of the intestinal wall beta-carotene is converted to retinol. This retinol, plus that absorbed directly from the food, is then re-converted back into retinyl esters. In this esterified form the vitamin A is carried in the blood, mainly as retinyl palmitate. Once it reaches the liver and kidneys the vitamin is stored as retinyl palmitate and released into the blood as free retinol when required. In the blood, the free retinol is complexed with proteins which keep it in solution.

When pure retinol is eaten, some 80% of it is absorbed. Of this absorbed vitamin, between 30% and 50% is stored in the liver. A further 20% to 60% is excreted in the bile which eventually finds its way back to the intestine. The remaining 10% to 20% appears in the urine as excretory forms of those active metabolites of the vitamin that are soluble in water.

Studies carried out in Britain by Drs T. Huque and A. S. Truswell, and reported in the proceedings of the Nutrition Society in 1979, indicated that the livers of well-nourished people killed in accidents contained as much as 400 mg (or 1,332,000 i.u.) of vitamin A. This would meet most people's requirements for at least two years if they were completely deprived of the vitamin. However, even liver supplies are not inexhaustible. In post-mortem surveys carried out in the USA and Canada it was found that between 20% and 30% of people had liver contents of vitamin A between zero and one-seventh of normal values. In Bangladesh, 78% of those studied had liver concentrations below one-seventh of those expected in well-nourished people. These figures illustrate that, nutritionally speaking, even those in the West are by no means replete in vitamin A.

A later study in 1982 looked at the liver reserves of vitamin A in 364 people who underwent post-mortems in London. Dr T. Huque reported in *The British Journal of Nutrition* that retinol stores ranged from zero in an 86-year-old woman who had died of cancer to 1201 mg/kg in a 22-year-old female who had committed suicide. About half the subjects had normal reserves within the range of 100-300 mg/kg which confirms the earlier study mentioned which claimed 270 mg/kg liver. However, 5% of those studied had extremely low reserves of under 40 mg/kg and a further 11% had very high reserves of over 500 mg/kg.

In this study, however, it was possible to compare liver reserves of vitamin A between those dying of natural causes and those who had suffered accidental death. There was a tendency for the people dying of disease to have lower liver concentrations than the other group. In fact, this reduction was of the order of 25% to 50%. Although this was partly explained by the fact that people dying of disease were in an older age group – it is known that vitamin A reserves decrease with age – the fact remains that on the whole disease does tend to lower the vitamin A level in the liver.

Previous studies by T. Moore at Cambridge indicated that the average liver concentration of vitamin A in accident victims was only 66mg/kg in 1937. The average figure of 270mg/kg determined in the 1982 study strongly suggests that over the intervening four decades, vitamin A status of people living in London has improved dramatically. Presumably the rest of the population is also showing this satisfactory increase.

The Functions of Vitamin A
Vitamin A has many functions within the body as evidenced by the manifestations of its deficiency. The tissues affected by lack of the vitamin include the eyes, the skin and the mucous membranes. Resistance to infectious disease is also lowered. We will now look at what is known about the functions of the vitamin.

Its Function in Sight
The best documented and understood function of vitamin A is in the process of low intensity vision. The light-sensitive cells of the retina are of two types, called rods and cones. Rods are concerned with low intensity or dim light vision. Cones function in high intensity light vision. Since colour can only be discerned in light of fairly high intensity – for example red and blue cannot be distinguished in dim light – it is generally recognized that the cones of the retina are concerned with colour vision. It is the lack of cones in the retinas of some animals, e.g. dogs and bulls, that leads us to believe that these species see everything in black and white.

Retinol is essential for vision in dim light. Only about one per cent of the daily intake of vitamin A is used by the retina, which receives and transmits to the brain the image formed by the lens. When the vitamin is lacking, the individual suffers from night blindness which reflects the eyes' inability to adapt to the dark or low intensity light. This complaint of night blindness is one of the oldest diseases known to man. Translations of ancient papyruses in Egypt indicate this, and they also give the cure – which was eating raw liver. However it was not until the twentieth century that this empiric treatment was shown to be due to the vitamin A in that liver.

We are all aware of the phenomenon of dark adaptation. The eye can adjust its response to nearly every degree of light by controlling the amount that falls on the retina through altering the diameter of the pupil. Hence, when entering a darkened room from a brightly lit environment there is always a short period of blindness followed by an increasing ability to discern objects in the dark, as the eyes adapt to the changes in light intensity. The eyes can adjust to as much as 90% of normal vision within a few minutes when the retina contains sufficient vitamin A. In deficiency of the vitamin, however, this period of adjustment becomes much longer – hence the descriptive term 'night blindness'.

How does vitamin A function in this process? The answer lies in its role in the photo-sensitive pigment of the retina. The rods, which we have seen are concerned with low-intensity vision, contain the pigment called rhodopsin (or visual purple), which is a complex of the protein opsin, and retinal (visual yellow), which is an active form of retinol. When light reaches the retina it splits the complex rhodopsin into its two constituents, opsin and retinal. The act of splitting rhodopsin causes nerve impulses to travel down the optic nerve to the brain, which converts them to the image that is seen. The more light that enters the eye, the faster the breakdown of rhodopsin.

In order to maintain vision however, there must also be a means of recombining opsin and retinal, and in normal circumstances this happens quickly so that the next light falling on the retina will again cause the breakdown of rhodopsin. Hence, the process of normal sight is a constant cycle of the breaking down and building up of this essential pigment rhodopsin. Light also converts the shape of the vitamin A as retinal from what is known as an 11-cis form to the all-trans type. Unfortunately, the all-trans retinal cannot combine with opsin to reform the complex rhodopsin. Before it does so, another mechanism comes into play whereby this all-trans retinal is converted back to the 11-cis type. In this form, it readily recombines with the protein opsin, and the process takes place in the dark.

Vitamin A as retinal thus has a central role in the process of sight in the light-sensitive rods of the retina. Probably it also plays a similar role in the high intensity-responding cones, but in these cells there may be a different kind of opsin. Naturally, in this constant degeneration and regeneration of rhodopsin there are bound to be small losses of the vitamin A component. If these are not replaced, an insidious deficiency develops and eventually the formation and breakdown of rhodopsin is curtailed. Once this happens, the time intervals for these processes increase and the bleached rhodopsin takes longer and longer to regenerate and night blindness results.

Obviously anyone who requires good night vision, such as airline pilots, lorry-drivers and ship's lookouts, must have sufficient vitamin A in the diet. It has been proved that the glare from the headlights of an oncoming car rapidly breaks down rhodopsin to such an extent that at 50 m.p.h. the average driver travels 73 feet comparatively blind. If the same driver is deficient in vitamin A this temporary blindness can extend two or three-fold. It must also be realized, however, that there is an optimum level of vitamin A required by the retina, and going above this by over-zealous intakes of the vitamin will not produce 'super sight'.

Its Function in Protein Synthesis

When we eat protein in our diets, the digestive processes break it down to its constituent amino acids which are then absorbed. The body then uses most of these amino acids as building blocks to produce its own proteins. These are utilized in the building and repairing of body cells, tissues and organs; in the mechanisms that prevent infection and in maintaining internal equilibrium in body fluids such as the blood so that excessive water is not retained. Vitamin A appears to have a prime role in the synthesis of the body proteins that are required for these functions. Animal experiments reported in *Nutritional Metabolism* (volume 15, 1973) indicated that when only small amounts of vitamin A are present, protein synthesis takes precedence over the other functions of the vitamin. When it is absent, protein synthesis stops.

These experiments have been confirmed in the main during observations on children who were suffering from protein deprivation leading to a disease called kwashiorkor. One manifestation of this condition is an increased occurrence of eye complaints, leading eventually to blindness. What happened in these children was that, when fed ample protein to overcome this deficiency, the eye diseases persisted. The reason was that there was no parallel increase in vitamin A intakes because the protein source was devoid of the vitamin.

Hence it was observed that increased protein intake also increased the need for vitamin A. One aspect of vitamin A function is that it is absolutely essential for growth in young animals, including human beings. Its function in protein assimilation would explain why vitamin A is needed for young body development and why normal growth continues only when both nutrients are present.

How the vitamin helps in building up protein has been elucidated by Dr T. R. Varnell of the University of Wyoming and reported in *The International Journal of Vitamin Nutrition* (1972). When rats were fed protein but deprived of vitamin A, their livers were found to contain excessive amounts of amino acids. Apparently, the liver was not capable of building up these amino acids into the protein required for its usual functions. Vitamin A is therefore a necessary tool to help construct those proteins in the organ that is the powerhouse of their production. Those rats fed adequate vitamin A with their protein demonstrated no increase in liver amino acid concentrations. Other animals developed low blood levels of protein in the absence of the vitamin, but these became normal on supplementation with vitamin A.

What we can conclude is that, if our diets are low in protein, efficient utilization of the nutrient will only happen if vitamin A is also present. Similarly as protein intake increases, so must the vitamin A in the diet.

High protein diets without accompanying vitamin A will cause a liver build-up of amino acids, just as in the experimental rats. We know from the kwashiorkor studies that, in man, vitamin A deficiency and protein malnutrition occur at the same time. The absorption of the vitamin is impaired when the diet lacks sufficient protein. This relationship between the two nutrients means that it is important that high protein diets, popular today as part of some slimming regimes, are supplemented with adequate vitamin A. Such diets may well lack the vitamin since oils and fats are usually avoided by slimmers.

Its Function in Resistance to Infection

During the period of intense study that followed the isolation of vitamin A, it gained a reputation as the anti-infection vitamin. This was based upon observations that the liver reserves of those dying from infections were invariably reduced. Usually blood levels of vitamin A were also found to be below normal in infectious diseases. These findings do not necessarily mean that the vitamin is lost by infection, but there could be a re-distribution of it, perhaps because it is diverted to the site of infection. Nevertheless, if vitamin A congregates in one part of the body other parts of it must be deprived. Adequate reserves will prevent this temporary, localized deficiency and its possible consequences. On the other hand, laboratory animals that were vitamin A deficient quickly fell victim to any infective organism present in the environment. Control vitamin-deficient animals that were kept in sterile conditions survived for longer periods.

These experiments were reported from the U.S.A. in the journal *Science* in 1969 and confirmation came from Dr T. Moore of the University of Cambridge in the U.K. He noted that in vitamin A deficiency the outer layers of tissues became weakened so that invading bacteria and viruses had easy access. The tissues most affected were those of the respiratory, urinary and intestinal systems. Hence pneumonia, urinary infections and enteritis were the commonest causes of death in the absence of vitamin A.

According to many researchers, vitamin A has no anti-infective property in its own right, but simply toughens up the tissues which mark the first line of defence against invading micro-organisms. Apart from the skin, the most vulnerable tissues are the mucous membranes, the wet surfaces of the body. According to Professor L. M. Deluca speaking at a symposium in 1968, vitamin A promotes the growth of mucous-secretory cells in epithelial tissue, that is the mucous membranes lining the respiratory, gastro-intestinal and urinary tracts. These membranes contain substances that protect against infection and also supply a physical barrier in the form of cilia, the tiny hairlike structures that line these areas of the body. Optimum health of these protective membranes is only achieved when vitamin A levels are adequate.

Another part of the body where vitamin A may influence resistance to bacteria and viruses is the thymus gland, whose function it is to develop resistance to disease. It is particularly important in the new-born and children, because it is at this stage of life that the cells specific for conferring immunity against attack by micro-organisms are really developed. The thymus acts as a central depot, dispensing antibodies throughout the body. As an individual grows older the thymus gradually loses its activity and dwindles in size. At one time this was thought to be due to the natural process of ageing, but more recent studies suggest that shrinking of the thymus may be more a result of stress and perhaps vitamin A deficiency.

The evidence for these relationships has come from studies at the Albert Einstein Medical College·in New York. Dr E. Seifter demonstrated that when mice were put under stress, the thymus reduced in size dramatically. At the same time there was enlargement of the adrenal glands – and the cortisone that is normally produced by these organs was present in excess to such an extent that the resistance-producing cells of the thymus were destroyed. It is an established fact that stress conditions lower a person's resistance to infection and diseases, and it was postulated that the destruction of the thymus by stress hormones like cortisone is one factor.

The role of vitamin A was suggested in the same studies to be that of a protecting agent against thymus shrinkage. Mice that were given large intakes of the vitamin under the same stressful conditions maintained normal thymuses. Hence, it looks as though we can place vitamin A alongside the vitamin B complex and vitamin C as nutrients that are required in extra amounts during stressful periods. Through its action in helping maintain a fully functional thymus gland, vitamin A is contributing in another way to its role as the anti-infection vitamin.

Low environmental temperatures, like those encountered in the winter months, represent another source of stress that appears to upset vitamin A metabolism. Winter, too, is the worst time of the year for developing respiratory infections and we have seen that adequate vitamin A is essential to help ward them off. A number of studies have looked at the relationship between vitamin A and low environmental temperatures and one of these was described in *The Journal of Nutrition* in 1967.

Once the weather gets colder the body is less able to utilize its reserves of vitamin A so dietary requirements for it increase. This was proved by comparing liver contents of the vitamin in rats living at various temperatures. As temperatures dropped, liver reserves increased. At the high environmental temperatures growth was far above that in the colder conditions, indicating a greater utilization of the vitamin in the growing process. There is no direct action of vitamin A in combatting the effects of the cold – rather it appears to work through the thyroid and adrenal glands. The thyroid controls the metabolic rate of the body, while the adrenals produce the hormones required to stand up to stress. However, neither of these glands will function effectively without adequate vitamin A. Its most likely function is in the synthesis of the hormones elaborated by these glands.

It is interesting to note that, of the rats exposed to the cold, none survived when injected with only 2.5 micrograms of vitamin A and at an intake of 10 micrograms seventeen per cent survived. None of these thrived at the low temperature but at an injection level of 100 micrograms not only did all the rats survive but they grew normally as well.

Similar observations have been made on children. It is known that they grow at a slower rate during the winter season, essentially because at lower temperatures vitamin A is retained in the liver and less is distributed to maintain growth. This applies only if the vitamin intake is the same during winter as in summer, but by supplementing during cold weather blood levels are kept high and sufficient vitamin A becomes available for its systemic functions. As well as growth, of course, this extra vitamin A helps induce resistance to infection as we have seen previously.

Its Function in Maintaining Healthy Skin and Bones

One of the first tissues to be affected by vitamin A deficiency is the skin, the epithelial tissue that covers the whole of the body. The outer cells on the surface and those in the lower layers shrivel up, lose their elasticity and die. The appearance is one of scaling, and because the dead cells break up into flakes they readily block up the pores of the skin preventing a normal exchange of nutrients, oxygen and skin oils. This rough and dry skin is not healthy and, because of this, it becomes susceptible to infection resulting in pimples, boils and other unwanted blemishes. Hence, vitamin A is required to maintain the skin's integrity – but it now looks as though it does not function alone. The mineral zinc is also essential.

According to Dr M. D. Altschule of the Harvard Medical School, there is ample evidence that vitamin A is required for collagen synthesis. Collagen is the ubiquitous protein of the connective tissues, including the skin, cartilage and bone. At the same time it is well established that zinc is required for vitamin A to be released from the liver, although the exact mechanism is not known. Hence both the vitamin and the mineral must be present in adequate quantities for the efficient healing of wounds, both traumatic and surgical, of ulcers and of skin complaints and indeed any problem requiring increased collagen synthesis. It is for this reason that supplementation with vitamin A and zinc has sometimes helped clear up skin complaints like acne, eczema and psoriasis.

Vitamin A also functions in normal bone growth and maintenance. Bone is a living tissue and like any other it is constantly being broken down and regenerated. The deposition of new bone is under the control of specialized bone cells called osteoblasts. The degeneration or dissolving of old bone is controlled by another set of specialized bone cells called osteoclasts. Usually there is a balance between the two activities, so that bone cells die off and are replaced smoothly. However, when vitamin A deficiency was induced in animals, according to Drs J. M. Navia and S. S. Harris reporting in the *Annals of the New York Academy of Science*, 1980, there was a reduction in the breakdown of bone tissue by osteoblasts. The net result is a bulky overgrowth of bony tissue and the failure of absorption of previously formed bone. Further investigation using tissue culture methods indicated that vitamin A actually causes both destruction and resorption of bone. The vitamin thus has an important role in healthy bone maintenance. The exact mechanism is unknown and it may well function via the parathyroid glands which are known to control calcium and hence bone metabolism. This recent knowledge does, however, raise hopes of treating intractable bone complaints like Paget's disease, according to publications in *Lancet* (1982).

Its Function in Preventing Anaemia

A six-nation Central American study has linked low levels of dietary vitamin A to widespread anaemia in children and nursing mothers in developing countries. This significant finding was reported in the *Medical Tribune* in 1981. Dr Luis Antonio Mejia of the Institute of Nutrition, Central America and Panama, told the conference that nutrition surveys in Central America have indicated that 20% to 50% of children in rural areas have endemic anaemia with very low blood vitamin A levels. Iron intake was adequate but the children appeared not to be able to mobilize it in the absence of the vitamin.

Supplementation with vitamin A was started by adding it to sugar lumps at a rate of 15 micrograms of retinol (about 50 i.u.) per sugar lump. The blood vitamin A increased three-fold and, although the average daily intake of iron remained the same, blood levels of the mineral increased. Eventually the anaemia disappeared.

It is believed that vitamin A affects the levels of the iron carrier protein in the blood. It functions, therefore, in releasing stored iron and making it available for blood formation, a process that takes place in the bone marrow. This particular type of anaemia may be more likely associated with an inability to absorb fat, which is one way vitamin A deficiency can develop even with adequate quantities in the diet.

Its Function in Reproduction

Many experiments on animals and studies on human beings over the past 25 years have indicated to the researchers involved that there is a direct link between vitamin A and sexual development. In the mature animal, vitamin A is required for the normal process of reproduction and subsequent growth of the fertilized egg. The vitamin is absolutely necessary for the production of normal, healthy spermatozoa in the male of the species, probably by virtue of its role in the synthesis of male sex hormones by the testes. Healthy female reproductive organs, and the ability of the female to accept and develop a normal fertilized egg, are also dependent on adequate body levels of the vitamin.

When experimental laboratory animals like mice, rats, hamsters and guinea pigs were made vitamin A deficient deliberately, all the males were characterized by undeveloped, shrunken and flabby testicles, according to Dr T. Moore of the Dunn Nutritional Laboratory in Cambridge. It was possible to reverse these changes simply by giving vitamin A, and the resulting reproductive glands resembled those of healthy animals fed a good, nutritious diet.

When the females of the species were treated in a like manner, deficiency of vitamin A resulted in lack of sexual interest. In those that did couple, however, there was an inability to conceive in most cases. Where conception did take place there was inevitable abortion of the foetuses. Once the females were treated with adequate oral vitamin A the full, healthy reproduction and foetal development processes were restored.

Earlier studies had indicated the essential function of vitamin A in maintaining normal spermatozoa in men and in boars. Dr A. Narpozzi, in the Italian medical journal *Rivista di Ostetricia e Ginecologia*, reported in 1954 that vitamin A deficiency in men reduced dramatically the quantity and mobility of their spermatozoa. Such abnormal sperm lowers their fertility and often leads to sterility. Only after vitamin A levels were returned to normal did the sperm take on the characteristics of the healthy variety and fertility was restored. This study was only part of a much wider one that was investigating many dietary factors in the maintenance of normal sex cells but it indicated the prime importance of vitamin A in this function.

Similar conclusions were reached in a study of boars by Dr B. Pallundon of Copenhagen. In the journal *Nature* (1966) he described how a vitamin A deficient diet in these animals caused a slow-down or even complete cessation of sperm production. When the vitamin was administered orally, complete normalization of sperm production was restored within three months. These studies, of course, are of supreme importance to anyone engaged in animal husbandry and breeding since they indicate how essential the vitamin is for the reproduction process, and the necessity for adequate vitamins in the diet.

Sometimes even the diet is not sufficient. Studies at the University of Purdue, U.S.A. have indicated that injections of vitamin A consistently improve the fertility of cows and the subsequent weight gain of their calves after birth. During the summer months the cows feed on bush grass, rich in the vitamin A precursor beta-carotene, and stores of the vitamin are laid down in the liver. Even these, however, are not sufficient to ensure adequate supplies of the vitamin throughout the winter months to satisfy the needs of pregnant cows. The diet appears to be inadequate, so ample supplies are obtained only from injection of the fat-soluble vitamin.

How does vitamin A contribute to the reproductive process? It appears to act in two ways. First by ensuring adequate production of sex hormones and second by an apparent direct effect upon the cell lining of the female reproductive tract. It must be said, however, that it is possible that the sex hormones are responsible for maintaining normal cell linings so these suffer from vitamin A deficiency by an indirect mechanism.

Research by Dr Isobel Jennings, reported in her book *Vitamins in the Endocrine Metabolism*, suggests strongly that the degeneration of the sex organs stems directly from an inadequate hormone supply, due to vitamin A deficiency. All sex hormones are produced by a series of biochemical conversions within the body from cholesterol, and vitamin A is known to be involved in at least two of the steps. In both male and female rats, for example, as vitamin A deficiency progresses so does the synthesis of the female hormones (the oestrogens) and the male hormones (the androgens) diminish. Once vitamin A is given, normal levels of the sex hormones are soon restored.

Degenerative changes in the cells of the testes that give

rise to spermatozoa (so-called germinal epithelium), were also noted in these animals when they were made vitamin A deficient. Although vitamin A restored normality, so did injections of the male sex hormone testosterone. These findings would therefore indicate that the primary protective and maintenance agents of the reproductive tissues are the sex hormones, but that vitamin A, in its turn, is essential in ensuring adequate synthesis of those hormones. Hence, lack of vitamin A in the male rat is equivalent to chemical castration, since the abnormal spermatozoa produced are incapable of fertilizing the female egg.

The effect of vitamin A deficiency on female rats was found to be just as serious in experimental studies. Conception in these animals is more difficult than in those with ample vitamin A, yet even when it is successful there are abnormalities such as a prolonged gestation period, problems in giving birth and usually death of the foetus. Birth defects include non-development of the eyes, cleft plate, and congenital heart disease.

These changes can be associated with a lack of female sex hormones, brought about, as in the male, by a block in their synthesis because of insufficient vitamin A. In addition, though, the cells lining the female reproductive tract become abnormal. The usual moist epithelial linings became hard and dry because of the formation of scaly cells. The process is known as keratinization, which is also characterized by a cessation of mucous production which normally keeps the linings moist and healthy. The dry, dead cells build up to form an impenetrable barrier that does not allow the free flow of nutrients. Similar changes are seen in the menopause of women, but here they are directly due to lack of female sex hormones which, in turn, is due to the degeneration of the ovaries rather than deficiency of vitamin A.

A connection between male diabetics and their greater tendency to impotence may be explained by the functioning of vitamin A in reproduction. In an article by Dr Alan Rubin in the journal M.D. (1968) he points out that the incidence of impotence in diabetic men can be as much as five times greater than in non-diabetic men. This is unlikely to be due to a direct effect of lack of insulin but appears to be related to the fact that diabetics are not able to convert beta-carotene to vitamin A efficiently. It is not known why this is so but it does mean that diabetics should look to foods containing pre-formed vitamin A for their needs. Recent recommendations by the British Diabetic Association suggest a decrease in fats in the diet of those suffering from diabetes. This in turn will reduce the availability of the fat-soluble vitamin A so it would appear to be a sensible precaution for anyone with diabetes to be aware of their need for the vitamin and perhaps look to supplements as a means of ensuring adequate daily intakes.

We have seen that in experimental studies on female rats, induced deficiency of vitamin A during pregnancy caused a higher incidence of birth defects in the offspring than in those rats replete with the vitamin. Female sex hormone levels increase dramatically during pregnancy and it is possible that when the vitamin is lacking, the ovaries and placenta are unable to supply the vast requirements of these hormones. The result is imperfectly developed foetuses that fortunately are often aborted spontaneously.

In human beings, the most critical period from the standpoint of congenital malformations is the first three months of pregnancy. Hence, it is during this time that a pregnant woman should look to her vitamin A intake. A letter from Dr R. W. Smithells of the University of Leeds suggests, in a recent *British Medical Journal* (29th January, 1983), that intakes of up to 10,000 i.u. are perfectly safe during pregnancy. There is evidence from various studies (M. Tolarova, *Lancet* 1982) that vitamin supplementation up to this level may reduce the incidence of cleft lip in human beings. This must be regarded as the limit of safety, however, even though studies on rodents by Drs D. H. M. Woollam and J. W. Millen (reported in *The British Medical Journal* 1957) indicated that only very high doses of vitamin A during pregnancy produced cleft palate and other defects in the offspring. On an equivalent basis a woman would have to take over five million units per day of the vitamin to reach the same intakes as those rodents. Nevertheless, it is sensible for any pregnant woman to ensure they reach at least a total daily intake of 10,000 i.u. to prevent any possibility of deficiency.

Vitamin A Deficiency

The observed effects of vitamin A deficiency vary widely from one species of animal to another. The general symptoms include loss of appetite, inhibited growth, increased susceptibility to infections leading eventually to death. The skin tends to be dry and scaly and the effect upon the scalp is reflected in poor hair production. Both the process of sight and the structure of the tissues around the eyes are abnormal in vitamin A deficiency leading to night blindness and xerophthalmia respectively. Night blindness has been discussed and the condition of xerophthalmia will be dealt with later. The respiratory tract in deficiency is characterized by a hardening of the lining cells with loss of cilia, the hair-like structures that keep mucous linings moist. Both of these result in multiple infections.

The mucous membranes of the digestive tract lose their elasticity in the absence of vitamin A and the secretory glands lining the tract cease to function. One consequence of this is increased susceptibility to infection. The absorption of nutrients from the digestive process become less efficient since some of them appear to be under the direct control of vitamin A. We have seen already how lack of the vitamin causes an overgrowth of bone, leading in some areas to nerve compression.

In some species there is a greater tendency to kidney stone formation with low body levels of retinol. The reproductive system also may be affected. In fowls, for example, deficiency leads to severe degeneration of the ovaries with a decline in egg production and fertility. In the males of the species there is degeneration of the cells of the testes resulting in lack of production of sperm. Both sexes demonstrate increased chances of infection in the genital systems. During pregnancy, a vitamin A deficiency is more likely to cause foetal abnormalities in a variety of animal species.

Despite all the manifestations of vitamin A deficiency that have been observed in animals, only some of them have been definitely associated with lack of the vitamin in man. This is not to say that the comparable symptoms in man have nothing to do with vitamin A, merely that possible associations have not been studied.

Xerophthalmia

We have seen that the first changes in the eye due to vitamin A deficiency result in an inability to see in the dark – the condition of night blindness. A more severe deficiency causes burning and itching eyes, inflamed eyelids, headaches and pains in the eyeballs. Eventually the disease known as xerophthalmia develops. Xerophthalmia is defined as a drying and degenerative disease of the cornea of the eye.

In its mild and early form, the conjunctiva (inner lining of the eyelid) dries up and hardens. As each layer of cells is affected, more and more build up into heaps of dried tissue that forces the eyeball out of its socket giving rise to the appearance of 'pop-eyes'. Tear secretions stop, infection sometimes sets in and ulceration results. As long as the xerophthalmia is confined to the conjunctiva there is no effect upon sight, but it is an early warning of the next stage which is blindness. This happens when the cornea, the clear area in front of the lens of the eye, becomes ulcerated and the cell changes seen in the conjunctiva affect this part of the eyeball. Naturally, vision is affected, but as a greater degree of deficiency develops the cornea becomes softened and takes on a bluish, milky appearance. It is insensitive to touch. Eventually the cornea starts self-dissolution, holes appear and the lens becomes exposed. The whole area then becomes open to infection and once this stage is reached permanent blindness is inevitable.

Xerophthalmia remains one of the main causes of blindness in the world today. It is a major problem in Indonesia, Bangladesh, southern India, parts of the Philippines and Thailand and in Sri Lanka, Afghanistan and Nepal. It still occurs in Latin America and in some parts of Africa. A World Health Organization study puts the number of people blinded by vitamin A deficiency into millions, mainly children. In many cases the disease is associated with protein-energy malnutrition (PEM).

Whilst the disease is still in the stage when it can be treated, doses of 30mg of retinol (100,000 i.u.) daily are given orally and by injection for at least 3 days followed by 9mg of the vitamin orally. Once the disease starts to respond to this treatment, further prevention is maintained by six-monthly injections of 60mg (200,000 i.u.) in an oily solution. This technique allows a slow, prolonged release of the vitamins to keep up blood levels. In Guatemala, table sugar is fortified with a water-soluble type of vitamin A and this approach appears to be working.

In the Philippines, supplementation is being carried out by fortifying monosodium glutamate with vitamin A. This flavour-enhancing agent is in wide use in that country and preliminary results suggest that this approach is successful.

Vitamin A and Cancer

The relationship between vitamin A and cancer was first noted in 1925 when it was reported in *The Journal of Experimental Medicine* that deficiency of the vitamin caused changes in cell differentiation in the epithelial tissues of animals, leading to cancer. Those apparently healthy animals who had low body levels of vitamin A were more susceptible to the formation of tumours than those with adequate retinol. Epidemiological studies (i.e. observation of specific groups) have suggested that low vitamin A or pro-vitamin A (i.e. carotene) intake may also increase susceptibility to cancer in man. A typical one was a 5-year follow-up study of 8278 men in Norway. Here, the incidence of confirmed lung cancer and glandular cancers was 4.6 times higher in men classified as having low vitamin A intake. This difference was statistically highly significant and independent of smoking habits. Other studies of blood vitamin A levels, measured as retinol, have demonstrated lower levels in patients with cancer than in control persons without cancer.

How can vitamin A function in protecting against cancer? To understand this we must first differentiate between tissue types and their prevalence to cancer. Normally, the external parts of the body and its entrances and exits (mouth, pharynx, anus and vagina) are lined by cells that make up the so-called squamous epithelium. On the other hand the gastro-intestinal tract, lower respiratory passages, gall bladder and cervix are lined by another type of tissue layers called glandular epithelium. Sometimes normal glandular epithelium becomes squamous and when this change takes place there is increased risk of cancer development. This was confirmed when it was shown that in foetal tissue, and to a lesser extent in mature animals, vitamin A deficiency predisposes to squamous epithelium in what is normally the glandular type. Adequate levels of vitamin A intake protect the animal against this change. At the other end of the scale, excessive levels of the vitamin encourage replacement of normally squamous epithelium by the glandular type – the complete reversal of the changes induced by vitamin A deficiency.

Certain substances are known to cause cancer in animals and in man, and they are known as carcinogens. Direct evidence of the value of vitamin A in protecting against cancer has come from experiments where intact animals were exposed to these carcinogens in such a way that they developed squamous cancer. When vitamin A was given in adequate quantity before exposure to such carcinogens, there was complete protection against cancer. It is known that a carcinogen induces cancer by becoming bound to the deoxyribonucleic acid (DNA) of the cells. DNA controls replication of cells and it is when this cell growth gets out of hand that a cancer results. Once bound to DNA the carcinogen stimulates the overgrowth of cells and the process continues uncontrolled in the absence of vitamin A. Adequate vitamin A, however, prevents the binding of the carcinogen to cell DNA and so neutralizes its cancer-inducing effect.

The main evidence of a relationship between suscept-ibility to cancer and vitamin A or carotene levels in the body has come from many epidemiological studies carried out worldwide. Recent work at Surrey University, Guild-ford and at Redhill Hospital has indicated a significant correlation between vitamin A concentration, the specific protein that carries the vitamin in the blood, and the amount of the mineral zinc that is present. When the blood of 26 newly-diagnosed lung cancer patients was measured for all three parameters, that of vitamin A was significantly lower than in a matched control group who did not have cancer.

A much larger survey, starting in 1975, was carried out as a joint study between Radcliffe Infirmary, Oxford and BUPA Medical Research and reported in *Lancet* (1980). In a prospective study of about 16,000 men who attended the BUPA Medical Centre for health screening, blood samples were collected and stored at deep freeze temperatures. By the end of 1979, 86 men were identified who had developed cancer. Another 172 control men who were alive and without cancer were selected from the remainder of the study population. These controls were chosen because of similar age and similar smoking habits and because their blood was taken at almost identica¹ times. Vitamin A levels were measured as well as other criteria, such as blood cholesterol.

What emerged from the study was that low retinol levels were associated with an increased risk of cancer. This association was independent of age, smoking habits and serum cholesterol levels and was greatest for men who developed lung cancer. Their vitamin A levels were only 187 i.u. per 100ml of blood compared with 229 i.u.

per 100 ml for the controls. The risk of cancer at any body site for men with retinol levels at the lower end of the scale was 2.2 times greater than for those with the higher levels. The conclusion reached was that measures taken to increase serum vitamin A levels in men may lead to a reduction in cancer risk.

A comparable study was carried out on 3100 patients in Evans County, Georgia in the United States. Low blood levels of vitamin A proved to be associated with an increased incidence of cancer that was independent of age and smoking habits. It was further found that those people who died of lung cancer invariably had lower blood levels not only of vitamin A, but of beta-carotene also, compared to those dying of non-cancer diseases. In these cases, it was also possible to measure the vitamin and its precursor in the liver, and again it was found that reserves of both nutrients were much lower in the cancer victims.

When we look at the relationship between a specific type of tumour, namely lung cancer, vitamin A intake and smoking habits, a more significant correlation emerges. A study by Dr E. Bjelke reported, in *The International Journal of Cancer* (1975), that when men were matched for equivalent tobacco smoking habits, those with a lower dietary intake of vitamin A had a higher incidence of lung cancer. The main dietary differences between the two groups was a higher consumption of carrots, milk and eggs in those people less prone to lung cancer. All these foods, of course, are excellent sources of vitamin A and carotenes. However, other findings emerged from the results. Dietary vitamin A was found to be inversely related to a five year risk of lung cancer among men who were current or former cigarette smokers. After allowing for the number of cigarettes smoked per day, men with lower levels of blood vitamin A, who also ate less quantities of vitamin A and carotene-rich foods, had more than 2.5 times the chance of developing lung cancer than those with good intakes of these micronutrients.

Since this report, similar inverse relationships between

dietary intake of vitamin A in its various forms and the risk of lung cancer – in other words the lower the intake the greater the risk – have been reported from studies carried out in the National Cancer Institute, U.S.A; among Chinese women in Singapore; among men studied in the U.K. and at the Roswell Park Memorial Institute in Buffalo, New York. In this trial, the dietary habits of 292 white male patients with lung cancer were compared with those of 801 white male patients with non-respiratory diseases and no cancer at any body site. The results again clearly indicated that those with lung cancer invariably had lower intakes of the vitamin in the diet which was reflected in lower blood serum values. To sum up, low retinol levels in the diet and in the blood are associated with increased risk of lung cancer.

The risk of cancer can be decided upon at birth if the hypothesis put forward by the Dutch doctor B. Dijkstra, based on his studies, is true. He reported in *The Journal of the National Cancer Institute* (1963) that when he investigated 330 consecutive patients in the Netherlands with proven primary cancer of the bronchus, those born in the winter had a risk of contracting this disease twice that of those born in the summer. He suggested that a reduced intake of fresh vegetables in the winter by the mothers or of fodder by the cows would produce a lower vitamin A content of milk. This could result in a depleted vitamin A diet for winter-born infants, thereby increasing squamous epithelium, at the expense of glandular epithelium, in these infants and perhaps rendering them more susceptible to bronchial cancer in later life.

The Western Electric Study

The most comprehensive study of the relationship between low dietary vitamin A and the risk of cancer was carried out on employees of the Western Electric Company in Chicago, U.S.A. The most significant finding was that beta-carotene, but not pre-formed vitamin A, decreased the risk of lung cancer. The report was published in *Lancet* at the end of 1981.

A total of 2107 men were examined in October 1957 and then again during December 1958. Questionnaires and a one hour interview were given to the volunteers at both sessions. Questions were asked about the kinds and quantities of foods and beverages eaten during the previous 28 days. It is interesting to note that vitamin supplements were so rarely used that any possible contribution was ignored. From food tables it was possible to calculate both the pre-formed vitamin A intake and that of carotene for each individual.

All the men participating in the trial were re-examined in this manner annually until 1969. Nine years after this the incidence of cancer over the 19 years following the start of the trial was assessed. The results were as follows. Men in the group that comprised the lowest 25% of carotene intake had seven times the relative risk of lung cancer as men in the group that made up the highest 25% of carotene intake. Among men who had smoked cigarettes for 30 years or more, the relative risk of developing lung cancer was eight times as great for men with low carotene consumption as for those with a high intake of the pro-vitamin.

After analysis of other nutrients in the diet, the authors of the study concluded that the key dietary variable related to risk of lung cancer is carotene. Pre-formed vitamin A and other nutrients provided by their diets were not significantly related to the risk of lung cancer. The long period of follow-up indicated that below-average intake of carotene preceded the development of cancer and was not a consequence of it. Also significant was the finding that neither carotene nor vitamin A intakes were significantly related to the risk of other types of cancer other than that of the lung.

The authors conclude that a diet relatively high in beta-carotene may reduce the risk of lung cancer, even among persons who have smoked cigarettes for many years. They emphasize, however, that cigarette smoking increases the risk of other serious diseases such as strokes and coronary thrombosis and there is no evidence that dietary carotene affects the chances of developing these.

Another study from Israel, reported in *The International Journal of Cancer* (1981), has compared the analysis of dietary data on 406 patients with gastro-intestinal cancer, and 812 people free of the disease, who were matched for age, sex, ethnic origin and length of residence in Israel. The study revealed no protective effect of retinol consumption against cancers of the gastro-intestinal tract. What was highly significant was the correlation between the consumption of carotene-containing foods and the decreased risk of cancer. The greater the number of carotene-containing foods consumed daily, the greater the decrease in cancer risk. Surprisingly though, when the daily carotene intake was calculated, there was no correlation between the absolute amount of carotene consumed and the cancer risk.

Hence these results confirm those of Western Electric, namely that only lung cancer appears to be prevented by carotene. The evidence, though, also implies that carotene-containing foods are beneficial in preventing gastro-intestinal cancer for reasons other than their carotene content. Perhaps people who eat lots of carotene-rich foods tend to eat less of other foods which may be more cancer-inducing. Several studies have indicated that fruit and vegetables appear to have a protective effect for both gastric and colonic cancers.

Therapy with Vitamin A

One of the metabolically active forms of vitamin A in the body is known as retinoic acid. This compound has all the properties of vitamin A except in relation to sight. It functions in growth and in the maintenance of healthy epithelial tissues but plays no part in the function of vision. This, we have seen, is confined to retinal or retinaldehyde.

Vitamin A and retinoic acid have both been used with some success in treating acne, eczema and psoriasis, by oral and topical (i.e. directly on the skin) routes and with and without ultraviolet light treatment. Although both retinoids (the term describes vitamin A and its derivatives) have reduced the incidence of cancers induced by potent carcinogenic substances in experimental animals, their use in human cancers has been limited by the fact that the potencies required to produce a beneficial effect are also those that cause serious side effects. These include headaches, lesions of the skin and mucous membranes, and liver injury. With careful dosage, however, retinoic acid has been used with very limited success in certain skin cancers, according to a report in *Lancet* (1980) by Drs N. Levine and F. L. Meyskens. Two patients were treated with 0.05% retinoic acid directly applied to the skin areas affected, under occlusive dressing. This was carried out daily. After 3 months treatment there was a complete disappearance of all skin lesions in one patient and a partial response in the other one. There were no side effects in either case.

The therapeutic ratio is described as the quantity of a retinoid required for a beneficial therapeutic effect compared with the extent of side effects. A high ratio is therefore desirable for any drug, and vitamin A derivatives are now being produced and studied which have therapeutic ratios ten or more times that of retinoic acid. Two such synthetic derivatives are 13-cis retinoic acid and Etretinate. They are not without side effects such as facial dermatitis, nosebleeds, conjunctivitis and a dry rash but they show great promise in replacing vitamin A and retinoic acid in therapy. The side effects preclude their general use and they remain prescription drugs only.

Vitamin A and Gastric Ulcers

Vitamin A has a protective effect on epithelial tissue, so it may have the potential for exerting a similar action against gastric ulcer. This hypothesis has been tested in a multi-centre, randomized, controlled trial of vitamin A in 60 patients with chronic gastric ulcers. The trial took place in Hungary and was reported in *Lancet* towards the end of 1982.

There were three groups of patients. One group was

treated only with antacids; the second group received similar antacids plus 150,000 i.u. of vitamin A; the third group were given the same doses of antacids and vitamin A as the second group but with the addition of cyproheptadine.

All patients were treated for four weeks. Ulcer sizes were measured before and after treatment in each case.

All ulcers were reduced to a significant degree, but the patients receiving vitamin A experienced a significantly greater reduction than those treated just with antacids. The authors concluded that 'a beneficial effect of vitamin A has been indicated in the prevention and treatment of stress ulcer in patients'. Gastric ulcer can be thought of as a pre-cancerous state, and significant negative correlation has been reported between the serum level of vitamin A and the development of lung, urinary, bladder and skin cancers. The results of this trial indicate a possible role for gastric protection in the prevention of the development of gastric cancer from gastric ulcer!

Vitamin A and Cortisone

One of the most common side-effects of oral cortisone, or indeed any corticosteroid treatment, is that any wounds or lesions of the skin that may occur during this therapy are very difficult to heal. Corticosteroid drugs are widely used in patients suffering from inflammatory diseases such as arthritis, gout, and rheumatic fever and in those with certain blood diseases, asthma and skin complaints. These drugs also act as suppressants of the immune system which protects us against bacterial and viral invasions so it is sometimes found that someone on long-term therapy is more susceptible to infections. At the same time, the normal healing response to injury is diminished. Hence, open wounds in people taking corticosteroids tend to heal poorly, so the risk of infection is enhanced and recovery is slowed down.

Recently, however, The National Institute of Health in Washington, U.S.A., announced that when vitamin A was applied directly to the open sores of patients who were receiving corticosteroids, the sores healed up. The research was carried out at the University of California, and healing was both rapid and complete. The wounds ranged from ulcers of the leg to severely infected chest lesions, and all had defied previous treatments. The surprising result was that some healed in a matter of days and all had disappeared completely within three weeks.

It must be stressed that the best response came from direct application of vitamin A to the wounds. When the vitamin was given orally, the response was not as dramatic. There was no response when similar treatments were tried on patients with recalcitrant wounds who were not on corticosteroid therapy. It is therefore possible that some reaction between the drug and the vitamin was contributing to the healing process. More likely however, is the possibility that the corticosteroids induced a localized deficiency of the vitamin in the area of the wound and the topical vitamin A, by circumventing intestinal absorption, overcomes this deficiency where it is needed. We know that vitamin A is necessary for healthy skin maintenance and resistance to disease, and a local deficiency would be expected to slow down the rate of healing of a wound.

Vitamin A and Derivatives in Skin Diseases

The effect of vitamin A on epithelial tissues has attracted much attention because its deficiency leads to hyper-keratosis (overgrowth of the outer skin cells) and to changes in the cells lining the wet tracts of the body. As we have seen, this latter aspect of deficiency may be a factor in the development of cancer.

Hyperkeratosis is a manifestation of many skin diseases including acne, rosacea and psoriasis. There is no hard evidence that these complaints are necessarily a conse-quence of vitamin A deficiency since, when small amounts of the vitamin are given to those suffering from them, the skin diseases do not always clear up. In addition, there is epidemiological evidence that populations that have widespread deficiency of vitamin A have no more prevalence to these diseases than those who have adequate vitamin levels. Nevertheless, with the knowledge that megavitamin therapy can often help relieve conditions that appear to be associated with deficiency, even when there is no evidence of it, it has been suggested that vitamin A and its derivatives could find a place in treating these and other skin complaints.

The anti-keratinizing properties of vitamin A are well established but when it was tried in high doses in acne, rosacea and psoriasis, its success rate was variable. At the same time, there were worries about possible side-effects from the megadoses used. In one trial, eighteen patients were given up to 200,000 i.u. per day for between 15 and 20 injections. This course was repeated three or five times and the results were promising. Symptoms disappeared in seven patients, improved substantially in nine and improved slightly in two. But side-effects appeared and their extent was such as to cause cessation of the trial after a few months. However, trials such as these did give benefit to some sufferers from skin diseases, so research was switched away from vitamin A itself to derivatives with similar or greater positive action but less side-effects.

It must be stated, however, that there are many anecdotal reports of the benefits of relatively low-dose supplementation of vitamin A (i.e. up to 10,000 i.u. daily) on acne, eczema and psoriasis and other skin complaints. The action of vitamin A is enhanced by simultaneous supplementation with the mineral zinc (up to 15 mg daily) probably because one function of this mineral is to ensure adequate uptake of the vitamin by tissues and its release from the liver.

Since acne often appears during puberty, it has been suggested that the sex hormones are involved in its development. We know that vitamin A is necessary for the natural production of sex hormones so it may be mediating through these. The oil of the Evening Primrose is another natural product claimed to help in clearing up mild skin complaints when taken at the rate of 150 mg daily. The mode of action of this oil is to supply precursors of other important body hormones known as prostaglandins. These too may have a role to play in normalizing skin cell formation and again their action may be mediated through vitamin A and zinc. The sensible way to approach self-treatment of these skin complaints is to ensure there is no deficiency of any of these factors. Supplementation at the levels recommended above will do this, and it is comforting to know that there is no harm at these potencies.

Retinoids

Retinoids are synthetic vitamin A derivatives that are produced by chemical modification of the vitamin. Some 1500 retinoids have been made and tested in biological systems since 1968. Their activity is assessed by measuring how well they protect the skin of mice against benign tumours induced by carcinogenic (i.e. cancer-producing) chemicals. A similar system enables diseases akin to those that cause hyperkeratosis to be studied. At the same time, the amount of the retinoid needed to cause symptoms of vitamin A excess is determined. The dose causing this toxicity divided by the amount required to stop the benign cancer or skin disease is calculated and designated the therapeutic index. In this way the derivative 13-cis-retinoic acid was found to be 2.5 times superior to all trans-retinoic acid (the natural form). Another retinoid, etretinate, had a therapeutic index ten times greater than the naturally-occurring all-trans retinoic acid.

Both retinoids, like vitamin A, influence proliferation and differentiation of the cells of the skin. They inhibit hyperkeratosis and reduce the production of sebum. Sebum is a natural secretion of the skin glands and its over-production is believed to be one of the factors giving rise to acne. Hence, anything that reduces the over-production of sebum would be expected to relieve that particular skin complaint, and this is precisely what happens. The oral retinoid 13-cis-retinoic acid is giving excellent results in severe acne, particularly the cystic variety, rosacea, seborrhoea and in hardening of the skin diseases. Etretinate has produced dramatic responses in severe, generalized psoriasis, particularly the refractory type that resists all other treatments.

We have seen that vitamin A, or preferably its precursor beta-carotene, is highly promising in the prevention and treatment of certain cancers, notably those of the lung and respiratory system. Retinoids show a similar beneficial action and are being studied in those people known to have a high risk of cancer, such as uranium miners, asbestos workers and heavy smokers. Etretinate is now known to prevent the further development of skin tumours in those suffering from them. Two excellent clinical trials have shown that this retinoid has a preventative effect on the recurrence of superficial bladder tumours. It also prevented the progression of lung cancer in heavy smokers according to a report in *Lancet* (1982). Other retinoids are being used successfully in research and in practice to treat many other types of cancer, mainly those of the skin, head, neck and mouth.

This concept of taking one of nature's products, vitamin A, and changing it to produce derivatives that are more active but less toxic than the vitamin is an exciting one. Preliminary results suggest that these retinoids may also find a place in the treatment of inflammatory and degenerative conditions like arthritis. They may also be used to control auto-immune diseases, where the body reacts to its own processes, by virtue of their action on the immune response. A further development is the possible use of beta-carotene in the prevention of some diseases, notably cancer, and perhaps in their therapy. The relative non-toxicity of beta-carotene makes it a potentially useful agent for treating these conditions, and it is possible that chemical modification of it may increase its therapeutic action.

The Toxicity of Vitamin A and Carotenes
Vitamin A is one of the more toxic vitamins, but there is a reasonable tolerance between the requirements for health and those needed to induce toxic symptoms. Toxicity can

be acute when an extremely high quantity is taken in one or a few doses. Chronic toxicity is a more insidious complaint and results from long-term intakes of the vitamin at potencies much less than those that cause acute symptoms, but rather more than those needed to maintain adequate body levels.

The oft-quoted acute toxic effects of vitamin A poisoning, experienced by Arctic explorers and whalers, include drowsiness, headache with increased cerebrospinal fluid pressure (this is the fluid that bathes the brain and spinal column), vomiting, extensive peeling of the skin and eventually death. Analysis has shown that the polar bear livers that were eaten by these people may contain up to 600 mg retinol per 100 g. Hence the intake of the vitamin was probably between 2 million i.u. and 20 million i.u. in one or two meals. As this represents between one thousand and ten thousand times the usual daily intake perhaps it is not surprising that this vast amount caused side effects. Although these cases are usually quoted when the toxicity of vitamin A is discussed, they are very unusual and bear no relation to everyday diets or even regular supplementation with the vitamin. Of more concern to those taking extra vitamin A is the chronic toxicity that may be induced by regular, long-term, excessive, supplementary intakes.

Since chronic vitamin A toxicity in children was first described in 1944, more than 50 cases have appeared in medical literature. Children, and particularly babies, who suffer this toxicity are usually the victims of misguided maternal enthusiasm, receiving a daily dose between 30 mg (100,000 i.u.) and 150 mg (500,000 i.u.) for several months. Sometimes concentrated preparations were given in amounts far above those suggested on the pack in the mistaken belief that if a little does good, more should do better. The characteristic changes observed were loss of appetite, irritability, a dry itching skin, coarse, sparse hair and swellings over the long bones due to excessive laying down of calcium. Sometimes the liver was enlarged.

A recent case reported in the medical journal *Paediatrics*

(January 1982) illustrates the effects of vitamin A poisoning in a 5-year old child. She was given capsules containing 25,000 i.u. of vitamin A and 1,000 i.u. of vitamin D to 'improve her eyesight' when she had measles. Over a period of several weeks, the girl was given about 50 capsules, providing a total intake of one and a quarter million i.u. She was admitted to hospital with swelling, peeling of the skin, headaches and vomiting. After only 5 days without supplement all symptoms disappeared and she was released.

A comprehensive study of vitamin A poisoning in 17 adults was made by Dr M. D. Muenter and his colleagues and reported in *The American Journal of Medicine* (1971). Most of them were women who had taken 14mg (46,000 i.u.) to 90mg (297,000 i.u.) vitamin A daily for over 8 years in attempts to cure chronic skin diseases. The clinical features noted were skin changes, headache, muscular stiffness and an enlarged liver. Once taken off the vitamin A supplements, all recovered over a period ranging from a few weeks to four months.

More recently a report in *The Journal of the American Medical Association* (March 1982) describes vitamin A toxicity in an adolescent following 'long-term, low-level intake' of the vitamin. The patient was a 16-year old boy who had taken 50,000 i.u. of vitamin A daily for two and a half years as a treatment for acne. He complained of headaches and nausea. Over a period of several weeks he had punctures to relieve fluid pressure that had built up in the skull causing the headaches. However, it took about eight weeks for his symptoms to clear up, despite being put on a vitamin A deficient diet.

The case is considered unusual since, as the authors point out, 'daily consumption of 50,000 i.u. of vitamin A by an adolescent would generally be considered safe. Literature reports of chronic hypervitaminosis A in teenagers have generally involved ingestion of 100,000 i.u. to 300,000 i.u. or more daily!' It does illustrate individual variation in the amount of vitamin A that will produce serious side effects, and the wisdom of keeping supplementation down to reasonable levels. The authors expressed concern about the ready availability (in the U.S.A. of vitamin A in unit doses of 25,000 i.u. per tablet or capsule and 'fear that an increase in cases of hypervitaminosis A may again occur owing to recent reports of profound beneficial effects of synthetic vitamin A compounds (retinoids) with various dermatological disorders of the skin and with certain types of cancer'.

We have seen that vitamin A functions in bone metabolism, and there are rare reports of excessive vitamin A intake causing mobilization of calcium from bone leading to high blood levels of the mineral. A typical case was published in *The American Journal of the Medical Sciences* (June 1982) from Columbia University, New York. A 55-year old woman had taken 75,000 i.u. per day of vitamin A for at least several months. At the end of six months she had lost 70 lb in weight and had multiple symptoms including weakness, bone pain, hair loss, dermatitis and smooth shiny skin with an orange hue. She was disorientated and psychotic and there was evidence of liver disease. Treatment was simply avoidance of vitamin A supplements.

Similar symptoms of excess calcium in the blood, associated with vitamin A toxicity, have been reported in *The British Medical Journal* (June 1981) in patients undergoing renal dialysis. It is recommended by the authors that vitamin A supplements should be avoided by anyone receiving this form of treatment.

In the United Kingdom and in some European countries, government legislation has restricted the daily dose of supplementary vitamin A in products allowed on general sale. Although 2,500 i.u. is the usual limit in food supplements, this may be increased to 7,500 i.u. per day in a product licenced as a medicine.

It must be remembered that a good diet will supply between 2,000 i.u. and 3,000 i.u. vitamin A daily so together with 7,500 i.u. as a supplement, a total daily intake of 10,000 i.u. is being supplied. This is ample for most people and it represents a safe, daily intake.

Carotenoids are much less toxic than vitamin A. When an individual regularly consumes very large amounts of foods rich in carotenes, the skin can take on a yellow colour, reminiscent of jaundice. Unlike jaundice, in which bile pigments accumulate in the body, the eyes do not become yellow and this represents a simple distinction between jaundice and hypercarotenaemia (excess carotene). Despite the high level of carotenes, however, no toxic symptoms have ever been recorded. Withdrawing the carotene-rich foods leads eventually to loss of the yellow colour in the skin. Not much of the carotene is converted to vitamin A when it is taken in large amounts, so there is no chance of retinol toxicity when carotene levels build up in the body.

2.

D – THE SUNSHINE VITAMIN

Discovery

Rickets, the disease we now associate with lack of vitamin D, was first described by Dr D. Whistler in 1645. Cod liver oil had been regarded as a traditional folk remedy in Scotland as early as the eighteenth century, but it was not until the mid-nineteenth century that its specific use in curing rickets was reported by the Scottish Professor Hughes Bennet of Edinburgh. At about the same time, the famous French physician Rousseau began to use this oil in treating rickets.

The association between lack of sunshine and the development of rickets was suggested by Dr Palm in 1890, but it was not until 1919 that a cure of the disease was demonstrated by exposing the skin to ultraviolet light. At this time too, Dr E. Mellanby first demonstrated unequivocally, with his studies on puppies, that cod liver oil contains a fat-soluble vitamin that cures rickets. The isolation of the active vitamin from natural sources followed in 1930. Shortly afterwards, a similar vitamin was manufactured by irradiating yeast with ultraviolet light and vitamin D became available in the pure state. However, it took until 1969 before it was discovered that vitamin D does not act as such in the body, but has to be converted into an active hormone in order to treat rickets.

Sources

From food: The body receives its vitamin D from two sources; from the diet and by synthesis in the skin. Only a very few foods provide vitamin D, and some contents are shown in Table 3. The only rich sources are the liver oils of fish, but these tend to be used as supplements of the vitamin rather than as normal items of the diet. It is interesting to note how fish accumulate such large amounts of vitamin D in their livers. They ingest plankton,

Table 3

The Vitamin D Content of Foods

FOOD	VITAMIN D mcg/100g
Cow's milk	0.03
Cow's milk – dried	0.24
Goat's milk	0.06
Butter	0.76
Cream – single	0.165
Cheese – hard	0.261
– cream	0.275
– cottage	0.023
Yogurt	Trace
Eggs	1.75
Cod liver oil	210.0
Margarine – all kinds	7.94
Liver – calf	0.25
– chicken	0.21
– lamb	0.50
– ox	1.13
– pig	1.13
Herring	22.5
Kipper	25.0
Mackerel	17.5
Canned salmon	12.5
Sardines	7.5
Tuna	5.8

minute organisms that live on the surface of the sea. These plankton contain vitamin D that has been produced by the action of sunlight on precursors synthesized by the organisms. Fish are not exposed to sunlight, so they rely upon this extraneous source of vitamin D for their needs. All vitamin D, therefore, must ultimately come from the action of sunshine upon inactive precursors.

Apart from fish liver oils, fatty fish in general are good sources of vitamin D. Less rich, but nevertheless useful, sources of the vitamin, are dairy products. Margarine as it is made is devoid of vitamin D but in most countries the vitamin is added by law, along with vitamin A, so the final product will provide meaningful amounts of both vitamins.

Human breast milk contains between 0.5 and 1.3mcg (20 and 52 i.u.) per 100ml, mostly as the water-soluble vitamin D sulphate. This is sufficient to prevent rickets, the vitamin D deficiency disease, in babies. Cow's milk contains much less of the vitamin, so infant's milk produced for bottle feeding is fortified with vitamin D.

From sunlight: The second, and in some cases, the more important source of vitamin D is the skin, where it is produced by the action of ultraviolet light upon sterols that have been deposited there by body processes. These sterols, or precursors, are synthesized by the body itself from cholesterol, and the most abundant is known as 7-dehydrocholesterol. This is as far as the body can transform cholesterol, and it requires light at a certain wavelength (290 to 312 nanometres) for the final conversion to vitamin D. The vitamin produced by this pathway is called cholecalciferol or vitamin D_3. The sterol 7-dehydrocholesterol is widely distributed in animal fats such as the oily secretions in mammalian skin and in the oil of the preen glands of birds. When dogs and cats lick their coats it is considered that this enables them to absorb the vitamin D formed there, as do birds when they preen their feathers. Milk also contains 7-dehydrocholesterol so it is possible to enrich it with cholecalciferol simply by exposing it to ultraviolet light. Unfortunately this treatment also destroys certain vitamins, notably riboflavin and vitamin A, so irradiation of milk is not to be recommended.

Many vegetables, along with yeast and certain fungi, are good sources of sterols that can act as vitamin D precursors, but it is only yeast that is exploited in their production. Irradiation of this sterol, called ergosterol, gives rise to several related substances of which only one, ergocalciferol, has vitamin D activity. This exposure to ultraviolet light has to be carefully controlled because some of the substances produced can be toxic, but modern techniques, combined with sensitive detection methods, ensure that only ergocalciferol is present in the final product. The other name for ergocalciferol is vitamin D_2 and, as far as the body is concerned, it is just as active as that formed within the skin.

Ergocalciferol is widely used in vitamin D therapy and in fortifying foods with the vitamin. It occurs very rarely in nature, being absent in practically all plant and animal tissues. It has a slightly different chemical structure to that of cholecalciferol, and the differences make separation and detection of each type of vitamin D (or calciferol) possible. This is extremely useful in research because the two can be differentiated in the blood. Hence, it is possible to compare the vitamin that comes from sunlight and fish oils (D_3) to that which is supplied from fortified foods and supplements (D_2). Such studies give valuable clues as to the importance of the two types of source in maintaining body levels of the vitamin and in preventing deficiency. One interesting fact to emerge from these investigations is that some people have no need at all for dietary vitamin D – their complete needs are met by the action of sunshine on the skin.

Biosynthesis of Cholecalciferol
The rate of synthesis of cholecalciferol in the skin is determined by the degree of exposure to ultraviolet light, but another factor is the pigmentation of the skin. Dr W. F. Loomis writing in the journal *Science* (1967) has suggested

that the control of skin colour over vitamin D synthesis has determined the distribution of the races of man throughout the world. It is generally believed that human beings originated in Africa, near the equator. The high intensity of solar illumination there would give rise to black skins due to excessive production of melanin, the colouring pigment of skin, as a protection against over-exposure. Black skins allow only between 3 and 36 per cent of ultraviolet rays to pass so these people would be more prone to rickets if they relied solely on the sun for their vitamin D.

As these people migrated north, the sunlight became less intense, and at the same time they were also less exposed to it because of the necessity to cover themselves with furs to keep out the cold. These heavily pigmented people, and particularly the children, became more susceptible to vitamin D deficiency because the rate of its synthesis was cut down. Even today black children in northern zones of the world are more susceptible to rickets than are white children in similar climes. Hence, as time progressed, natural selection would have favoured the evolution of people with fair skins. Members of the white races are transparent-skinned in winter when they need the maximum exposure to the low intensity light to produce their vitamin D. In the summer they tan, producing melanin which protects them against excessive ultraviolet light. This is sufficient for adequate vitamin D production but not enough to cause burning. White skin allows between 53% and 72% of the ultraviolet light to pass to those layers that contain 7-dehydrocholesterol, so vitamin D biosynthesis is much more efficient than in black skins.

In order to back up his hypothesis Loomis has attempted to quantify the amount of vitamin D synthesized in the skin. He calculated that the pink cheeks of a European infant – an area of about 20 square centimetres – can synthesize daily about 10 mcg of vitamin D if exposed to three hours of sunlight. This amount happens to be an infants' daily need, but there is no guarantee that that light intensity is sufficient for it throughout the year.

Recent studies have shown conclusively that the two main factors controlling the vitamin D status of the body are the intensity of skin pigmentation and the season of the year. The first trial was performed at Harvard Medical School and the Massachusetts Institute of Technology and reported in *Lancet* (1982). The aim of the trial was to determine the effect of increased skin pigment on the skin production of vitamin D by measuring the amount of vitamin D_3 in the circulating blood.

Two light-skinned Caucasian men and 3 dark-skinned Negro volunteers (one woman and two men) were exposed to a single dose of ultraviolet light in a walk-in irradiation chamber. Exposure of the Caucasian subjects to a minimum dose of light greatly increased the blood vitamin D concentration by upto 60-fold, 24 to 48 hours after exposure. Within seven days, however, the vitamin levels had reverted to those before irradiation. The blood concentration of vitamin D_3 was not changed by a similar exposure to ultraviolet light in the negro subjects. In fact, it took at least six times the dose of ultra-violet light to bring the blood levels of D_3 in those with dark skins to the same concentration as the single dose with the light-skinned subjects. The authors conclude that high concentrations of melanin in the skin reduce vitamin D synthesis but do not block it. They speculate that dark skin may further increase the risk of vitamin D deficiency in populations with low dietary vitamin intake and reduced exposure to sunlight.

An important study, indicating that the vitamin D status of the body in the winter is determined more by previous exposure to summer sunlight than by dietary intake of the vitamin, was reported by Dr E. M. E. Poskitt and colleagues in *The British Medical Journal* (1979). In 110 white West Midlands children, blood levels of vitamin D showed a pronounced seasonal variation, the values being highest in August and lowest in February. However, those children who had had a seaside holiday the previous summer had higher vitamin D concentrations in their blood than those who had not had a holiday away from home. There was no difference in daily dietary intakes of the vitamin, so the increase in blood levels must have been related to higher skin synthesis in those who had spent time at the seaside.

In a parallel study the vitamin D levels in the blood of 11 healthy adults in Cambridge were measured and those of the vitamin derived from the skin (D_3) were consistently higher than those of the vitamin from the diet (D_2). All subjects were then given 200 i.u. (5 mcg) of ergocalciferol daily (D_2) for 28 days and, although the concentration of this in the blood was increased, it did not reach that of cholecalciferol (D_3). This study, therefore, confirmed others from the U.S.A. and U.K. that had found that cholecalciferol from the skin is the dominating circulating form of vitamin D in the blood throughout the year. There is thus much evidence that, even in winter, the concentration of circulating vitamin D in normal people is determined largely by exposure to solar radiation during the previous summer and by the rate of skin-synthesized stores of cholecalciferol built up at that time.

Despite popular belief, domestic sunlamps and sunbeds do not contribute usefully to skin synthesis of vitamin D. A report in *The Postgraduate Medical Journal* of 1981 indicated that burning of the skin is highly likely to occur before any substantial rise in the blood concentration of chole-calciferol.

When Biosynthesis is Reduced

We have seen how skin pigmentation can reduce vitamin D synthesis but there are other factors that do so that are related to the environment. Pollution in the atmosphere contributes particles of dirt and grime that obstruct the ultraviolet rays needed to make vitamin D. Smoke from domestic and industrial fires used to be the main factor in inducing deficiency of the vitamin in urban populations. The introduction of coal-burning in the seventeenth-century Britain also coincided with the first recorded rickets epidemic. Things never got any better in the cities, and pollution probably reached its peak during the

Industrial Revolution and persisted into the 1930's. A report in the journal *Nature* (1974) by Dr T. P. Eddy of the London School of Hygiene and Tropical Medicine mentioned that during the period 1937 to 1939 in the industrial city of Leicester, diseases directly attributed to lack of vitamin D increased dramatically. At this time pollution from smoke was at its peak and studies indicated that the atmosphere prevented from 30% to 50% of ultraviolet light reaching the population. The weak light during the winter months was therefore virtually useless in producing vitamin D in the skin.

Clean-air zones and the introduction of smokeless fuel since that time have reduced atmosphere pollution considerably but not completely. Anyone who observes a city when approaching it from the air cannot fail to see a permanent haze over it, even today. Those of us in the northern latitudes who live and work in conditions of weak sunlight during the winter months will hardly receive enough light for biosynthesis of vitamin D. Brightly lit offices, works, factories, schools and shops will absorb the health-giving rays from sunshine. Housebound and bedridden individuals never get the chance to make their own vitamin D so they must rely on dietary sources.

Confirmation has come from studies conducted by Dr R. M. Neer of Harvard Medical School who published his results in the *Medical World News* (1971). Thirty-three men, aged between 52 and 93, who were permanent residents of an old soldiers home were studied for four-week periods during two consecutive winters. During the experiment they were confined indoors, away from windows.

One group was exposed to controlled lighting from fluorescent tubes at the same wavelength as ultraviolet light from the sun. The second group was exposed to the same intensity light for the same period, but from conventional fluorescent tubes. Vitamin D production was assessed by measuring the intestinal absorption of calcium, which increases in the presence of the vitamin.

Those who received ultraviolet radiation corresponding to sunshine had significantly increased calcium absorption during both periods of irradiation. The group exposed only to conventional fluorescent lamps showed a significant fall in calcium absorption during the period of irradiation. Both groups appeared to be healthy during the periods of experimentation but there was some evidence of possible deficiencies of vitamin D. Anyone who is housebound or bed-ridden for long, unbroken periods would therefore be advised to look to their dietary intakes of vitamin D to ensure they are adequate according to Dr Neer. These considerations apply to all age groups.

Stability in Foods

Vitamin D is generally regarded as being very stable in foods and during cooking processes, but the difficulty of measuring the tiny amounts present in food has restricted studies in this field. Commercial processing like smoking of fish, pasteurization and sterilization of milk, and the spray-drying of eggs, have little effect upon vitamin D levels. It is, however, a fat and any process likely to cause oxidation of fats will adversely affect the vitamin. In the production of infants' milk the vitamin is usually added in an excess of between 25% and 35% to provide for any destruction during the drying process.

Daily Requirements of Vitamin D

As most children should obtain the greater part of their vitamin D requirement from the action of sunshine on the skin, it is difficult to assess exactly their needs in the diet. We have seen, however, that for various reasons skin synthesis may not suffice so, in some cases, dietary intake determines whether a child is obtaining adequate vitamin D. In Britain, as in many countries, the authorities recommend a daily dietary intake of 10 micrograms. One microgram of vitamin activity is the equivalent of 40 i.u. so this intake can also be expressed as 400 i.u. daily. Studies in Britain have shown that, despite fortification of infant milks and other foods with the vitamin, many young children and infants receive amounts that are below this recommended allowance. The authorities are reluctant to increase the level of fortification because of possible side effects from overdosage, so many children whose dietary intake of the vitamin is inadequate require a supplement. Cod liver oil, either in liquid or capsule form, is the usual choice. Halibut liver oil, always in capsule form, is also popular but it must be remembered that the potency of vitamin D is much higher in this than in cod liver oil. The label should state clearly the potency of the vitamin D present whether it be per teaspoonful (5 ml) or per drops or per capsule or tablet so the intake can be calculated. It must be remembered, too, that in preparations available on general sale vitamin D is always accompanied by vitamin A in such a proportion that adequate, and not excessive, quantities of both are provided.

Older children and adults are believed to need less in their diets. From the age of seven years on, the recommended daily intake is 2.5 micrograms (100 i.u.). It is only during pregnancy and whilst breast feeding that an increased intake of 10 micrograms (400 i.u.) is recommended. These are the suggestions of the UK authorities. Other countries' advisors are more generous and in the U.S.A. and in Europe a daily intake of 400 i.u. throughout life is recommended. There is evidence that 100 i.u. is adequate to prevent deficiency in adults and 400 i.u. does not cause toxic side effects so a daily intake somewhere between the two figures is probably the ideal. In the U.K. suggested dosage of vitamin D supplements available to the general public is limited to 250 i.u. daily (6.25 mcg) in unlicenced preparations and 400 i.u. daily (10 mcg) in those with a DHSS product licence. Any potency above this is available only on prescription.

The Metabolism of Vitamin D

Vitamin D is a fat-soluble vitamin so, like any fat, it is absorbed from the food in the small intestine. The presence of bile salts is essential for its absorption because they are needed to reduce it to the tiny globules called chylomicrons. These are absorbed intact and as such the vitamin is carried to the liver attached to specific proteins in the blood. These same proteins carry the vitamin D that is formed in the skin (cholecalciferol) from that tissue into the bloodstream and hence to the liver.

For many years the vitamin was believed to act as cholecalciferol or as ergocalciferol but we now know that these are not the active forms. In the liver, both types are converted to the appropriate 25-hydroxy vitamin D (25-OH-D) (i.e. either D_2 or D_3) and this is the form of the vitamins that circulate in the blood. Usually the concentration in the blood plasma is above 5 micrograms per litre. The fatty tissues of the body represent a greater storage depot for vitamin D than does the liver. It is excreted in the bile as inactive metabolites.

The 25-OH-D is carried in the blood to the kidney where a further conversion takes place under the influence of enzymes to the 1,25-dihydroxy vitamin D (1, 25-$(OH)_2$-D). This is the active form of vitamin D and it is produced only in the kidney. When the kidney is not functioning correctly, as in renal diseases, this transformation is inefficient and it explains why one feature of such diseases is often an upset in vitamin D function.

The active form 1,25-$(OH)_2$-D (either D_2 or D_3) is some ten times more potent than the vitamin itself in its action on target tissues, and it acts much more quickly. In many studies it was noticed that there was a 10 to 12 hours delay before vitamin D exerted its functions and it was this observation that stimulated the search for a more active form. The goal was reached in Cambridge, by Dr E. Kodicek in 1974 and in Wisconsin, U.S.A. by Dr H. F. Deluca in 1976. The discovery of 1,25-$(OH)_2$-D opened up entire new frontiers in our knowledge of how vitamin D functions.

The Functions of Vitamin D
We know that vitamin D does not act as such but must

first be converted to 1,25-dihydroxy vitamin D and this compound has a hormone rather than a vitamin function. A hormone is defined as a substance synthesized in one part of the body that acts upon another part, the so-called target organs. Cholecalciferol is produced in the skin then converted by the liver and kidneys into the active 1,25-dihydroxy cholecalciferol which functions elsewhere in the body. Hence, cholecalciferol satisfies the criteria for a hormone. Since it can be synthesized in the body and need not necessarily be supplied in the diet, cholecalciferol does not satisfy one of the criteria for a vitamin. This intriguing suggestion was put forward by Dr W. F. Loomis in an article in *Science* (1967). It bridges the gap neatly between vitamin and hormone function and in this respect cholecalciferol is unique amongst the vitamins.

Vitamin D, as 1,25-dihydroxy vitamin D, functions as a hormone which, with two other hormones known as parathyroid hormone and calcitonin, regulates calcium and phosphate metabolism. Three metabolic effects of the active form of the vitamin have been identified.

(1) It promotes the absorption of the mineral calcium in the small intestine, by inducing the synthesis of a specific protein required to bind the calcium within the cells lining the intestine.

(2) It acts on bone, causing it to release calcium into the blood circulatory system where it can then be transported to where it is needed elsewhere in the body. This mechanism also requires the presence of parathyroid hormone.

(3) It facilitates the absorption of phosphate from the small intestine by a similar mechanism to that operating for calcium. This is independent of the calcium transport system, however, since it operates in a different part of the small intestine.

Whenever there is a fall in blood plasma concentration of calcium, synthesis of parathyroid hormone by the parathyroid gland is stimulated. In its turn, parathyroid hormone causes the transformation of 25-hydroxy-D into 1,25-dihydroxy-D within the kidney. Once this active form of vitamin D is released from the kidney it acts upon the intestine to absorb calcium from the food, and upon the bone to release the mineral and so plasma calcium increases. When the concentration of calcium rises to a certain level it has the effect of stimulating the production of the hormone calcitonin.

This in turn causes a decrease in parathyroid hormone synthesis. The net result is decreased assimilation of calcium, so the blood level of the mineral stays constant. As calcium is used its concentration in the blood gradually drops, and when it reaches a certain level the whole cycle of events starts again. A similar regulatory mechanism controls blood plasma inorganic phosphate concentration.

Deficiency of Vitamin D and its Causes

Deficiency of vitamin D during childhood leads to the development of rickets. Rickets is a word derived from the Anglo-Saxon, *wrikken*, which means to twist. The disease is characterized by a softening and deformity of the bones due to a lack of uptake of the mineral calcium. Calcium may be present in the diet but, because vitamin D is deficient, the mineral cannot be absorbed from the small intestine.

In adults, lack of the vitamin causes the disease known as osteomalacia, which means softening of the bones. The features that differentiate rickets from osteomalacia are due to the fact that in children, the ends of their bones are in a state of active growth. Hence, the bones continue to grow but they are not hardened by the deposition of calcium phosphate, and under the weight of the child they twist and bow to give the characteristic appearance of rickets. In adults, growth of the bones has ceased, so in osteomalacia the problem is mainly one of lack of absorption of calcium from the diet. In an attempt to maintain blood calcium levels, the mineral is withdrawn from the bones which become soft, weak and painful.

Although the disease was known for many years, it was not until the mid-seventeenth century that the spread of rickets reached alarming proportions. Its increase coincided with the development of industrial cities at that time. Chimney smoke and high tenement buildings combined to cut out the sunlight and, as we now know, this removed one of the prime sources of vitamin D. Before 1900, the incidence of rickets in children of the poorer classes was as high as 75% in the larger cities of the world, because lack of sunlight was not compensated for by increased dietary intake of vitamin D. Milk and dairy foods were beyond the reach of the poorer families and, as we have seen, there is no dietary source of vitamin D beyond those, apart from the more expensive liver and meats. The main item of these people's diets was cereals, and these exacerbated the lack of sunshine and dietary vitamin D by supplying large amounts of phytic acid. This acid immobilized the calcium in the diet, so lack of the mineral was yet another factor in the aetiology of rickets in those times.

Despite the discovery of vitamin D in 1918, it was not until 1923 that Dr Harrietta Chick and her colleagues, working in Vienna (which was a blackspot for rickets), demonstrated unequivocally that lack of sunshine and lack of the vitamin in the diet were both factors in the development of rickets. Thanks to these studies, the incidence of rickets in the West declined dramatically between the two world wars. This was due to an awareness of cod liver oil as an excellent supplement for children, coupled with increased exposure to the sun due to a programme of slum clearance and a reduction in industrial and domestic chimney smoke. Sunbathing became popular, in part due to a public awareness of the value of the 'sunshine vitamin', as vitamin D came to be called.

Rickets Today
The prevalence of rickets has been studied extensively in Glasgow because, even today, its incidence in that city is the highest in the U.K. Only ten or so cases are seen each

year but surveys of more than 4000 Scottish Infants, carried out by Dr G. C. Arneil (1975) indicated that up to 7 per cent of children aged 1 to 3 years have minimal rickets. Most reach school age without any bone deformities, so the effect of the observed levels of vitamin D in the blood is not certain. Other big cities in the U.K. have slightly lower incidences of rickets than Glasgow.

There are in Britain as many as 25 per cent of children whose dietary intake of vitamin D has been calculated as less than 100 i.u. daily. This is far below the recommended minimum of 400 i.u. The low intakes are reflected in the decreased blood levels of 25-hydroxy cholecalciferol which are usually at the danger level of less than 5 mcg/litre. Despite this, these children show no clinical signs of rickets, and X-rays of their bones appear normal. Nevertheless, they are regarded as suffering from hyprovitaminosis D (low body levels) and represent a high risk of developing rickets if their vitamin intake remains low during the growing years. Supplementation with cod liver oil appears to be the best insurance against developing the disease.

During the 1950's the children of Asian immigrants to Britain began to show clinical signs of nutritional rickets. In children of European origin this type of rickets is very rare beyond the age of 8, according to a *Practitioner* article by Dr G. C. Arneil in 1973, but Asians were appearing with rickets in adolescent children as well as the younger ones. This cannot be entirely due to their skin pigments, since the more heavily pigmented West Indian children are much less afflicted with the disease and, in fact, have an incidence no higher than white children in the same areas. One survey, reported by Dr N. Ruck in *Proceeding of the Nutrition Society* (1973), found that the average daily intake of vitamin D by Asian, West Indian and European children was estimated to be only 60 i.u., 72 i.u. and 64 i.u. respectively, figures that show no real significant difference. Hence, there must be other reasons why Asian children have a greater prevalence to rickets when in Britain, and one clue lies in the vitamin D status of pregnant Asian mothers.

In one trial, reported in *Lancet* (1975), Asian women at the time of delivery of their babies had an average blood plasma concentration of 25-hydroxycholecalciferol of only 7.6mcg per litre, a figure dangerously near that diagnostic of hypovitaminosis D. The corresponding figure for European women was 18.3mcg per litre.

A later review of 3327 deliveries in 1978 confirmed that blood plasma levels of 25-OH-D in Asian mothers were consistently low at the birth of their children. As many as 81% of the mothers and 30% of their babies had body levels consistent with osteomalacia in the adults and rickets in the babies. Other studies indicated that in general, adult Asians living in India had a much higher status of vitamin D than their counterparts living in Britain. It was concluded that the high frequency of rickets and osteomalacia among Asians in Britain can be explained by their low intake of vitamin D in the diet and inadequate solar exposure.

There are many more studies confirming the high incidence of rickets in growing children, and of osteomalacia in adult Asians, and much effort has gone into ways and means of combatting these vitamin D deficiencies. The culmination of this concern was a Working Party under the chairmanship of Dr Elsie Widdowson, one of Britain's top nutritionists, who reported their conclusions in 1980 in the document 'Working Party on Fortification of Food with Vitamin D. Committee on Medical Aspects of Food Policy (Rep. Health, Soc. Subj. No.19)'. They advised against fortification of food with vitamin D as a means of tackling the problem of rickets and osteomalacia in Asians living in Britain. The argument was a familiar one. Previous experience had shown that Britain had no sooner conquered rickets in its own population 40 years before there was an outbreak of infantile hypercalcaemia (too much calcium in the blood) due to excess vitamin D intake. The path between efficacy and toxicity of vitamin D is narrower than was originally thought. Individuals vary so much in their consumption of foods amenable to vitamin D fortification (chapatti flour was one possibility) that it was impossible to determine a safe level of constant fortification. The committee concluded that the safest courses were regular supplementation with the vitamin at the individual level and a programme of health education. It was also suggested that windows should be made of glass that will let in light at the wavelength necessary to allow formation of the vitamin in the skin, and that fluorescent lamps should be developed which emit a light that will also activate the vitamin in the skin.

Osteomalacia

Osteomalacia is the adult counterpart of rickets. It often affects women of child-bearing age who become depleted of calcium by repeated pregnancies. It was once very common in the Middle and Far East. The main factors included the purdah system (complete covering of the body and a restricted life indoors), cold winters and a poor diet with little or no milk and dairy products. In Europe the incidence of the disease paralleled that of rickets, and improved social and environmental conditions were factors in conquering both diseases.

Today osteomalacia is still an important disease in Asia, and it is not uncommon in elderly women in Scotland. It is still present in many northern countries where the winter sunlight is insufficient to allow adequate synthesis of vitamin D to make good a dietary deficiency. Particularly prone are old people who are housebound because of physical incapacity. Sometimes osetomalacia is complicated by osteoporosis, which is a honeycombing of the bone due to excessive loss of calcium. One study, reported in *Lancet* (1974), found that 34 per cent of women over 50 years of age with fractures of the femur showed features of osteomalacia. This is relatively easy to treat with calcium and vitamin D, but other factors are concerned in the development of osteoporosis, which sometimes accompanies osteomalacia, and this is far more difficult to treat.

Occasional cases of osteomalacia in younger women have been reported from several of the larger industrial cities in Britain. Most of them are of Indian and Pakistani origins and the disease is present more frequently in pregnancy. Many studies have indicated the value of supplementation at this time, usually at daily doses of between 400 and 1000 i.u. vitamin D daily. These doses also are sufficient to prevent deficiency of the vitamin in the new-born child.

Chronic diseases of the digestive system which prevent the absorption of fats are often the cause of osteomalacia. Vitamin D is fat-soluble and is best absorbed in the presence of fats, so it too is affected by these diseases. Osteomalacia also occurs in certain forms of kidney disease where the diseased organ is unable to conserve calcium and losses of the mineral are excessive. It is also possible that kidney failure results in the loss of ability of that organ to convert 25-hydroxy-D to 1,25-dihydroxy-D. The consequence is deficiency of the active form of the vitamin and decreased absorption of calcium.

Drugs used in treating epilepsy, known as anticonvulsant drugs, can induce rickets in children and osteomalacia in adults when they are on long-term therapy. Phenobarbitone and phenytoin are particularly active in this respect. The reason is that these compounds cause changes in the liver enzymes necessary to convert vitamin D to 25-hydroxy vitamin D. Instead of producing the required metabolite, inactive compounds are formed, so requirements for vitamin D are increased. Treatment is carried out by giving supplementary vitamin D or its metabolite 25-hydroxy vitamin D.

Symptoms of Vitamin D Deficiency

The infant with rickets has often received sufficient dietary energy and may appear to be well nourished. However, the child is usually restless, fretful and pale with flabby and toneless muscles which cause the limbs to assume unnatural postures. Excessive sweating of the head is common, weakened abdominal muscles that have lost their tone give rise to distension, which is increased by intestinal fermentation of undigested carbohydrates.

Gastro-intestinal upsets with diarrhoea are common. The infant or child is prone to respiratory infections. Development is delayed leading to late development of teeth and there is failure to sit up, stand, crawl and walk at the early stages. Bone changes represent the most specific symptoms of rickets, and these are characterized by thickening of the growing ends of the bones. As soon as the child can stand on its feet, deformities of the shafts of the leg bones develop, so that 'knock knees' or bow legs become an obvious feature. Rickets, as such, is not a fatal disease, but the untreated reachitic child is a weakling with an increased risk of infections, notably broncho-pneumonia.

In osteomalacia, pain is usually present and ranges from a dull ache to the more severe variety. The areas usually affected are the ribs, the lower vertebrae of the spine, the pelvis and the legs. Bone tenderness on pressure is common. There is often muscular weakness present, leading to difficulty in climbing stairs or simply getting out of a chair. Sometimes a waddling gait develops. Muscular spasms and facial twitching are the result of the low blood calcium levels that are a feature of the disease. The bones become brittle because of loss of calcium and spontaneous fractures are common.

Therapy with Vitamin D

The only diseases with an established therapeutic response to vitamin D are rickets and osteomalacia but benefits in osteoporosis and rheumatoid arthritis have also been claimed.

In treating rickets the usual dose is between 25 and 125 mcg (1000 to 5000 i. u.) per day, depending upon the severity of the disease. Children can be given halibut liver oil in a very small dose of 1 cc, because this oil contains 30 to 40 times the concentration of the vitamin of cod liver oil. In severe cases, the high dose of 125 mcg is usually met by using synthetic vitamin $D(D_2)$. In third world countries where medical care is available only occasionally, treatment consists of a single massive dose of vitamin D, usually 3.75 mg (150,000 i.u.) every six months or so. Fortunately, side effects are rare, probably because the child is so depleted of the vitamin that the liver and fatty tissues can accept and store this amount safely. Calcium is usually given at the same time, but this is far more effective if taken in the diet on a daily basis.

The treatment of osteomalacia follows similar principles. When the disease is due to simple lack of dietary vitamin D (combined with reduced synthesis in the skin), a daily intake of 25 to 125 mcg (1000 to 5000 i.u.) is sufficient to treat the complaint until symptoms disappear. Then a maintenance dose of 400 i.u. daily is given, along with dietary advice and exposure to the sun, especially if the cause of osteomalacia cannot be determined or removed. When the patient is unable to absorb vitamin D, because of an inability to absorb fats, a much higher dose is required. A daily intake of up to 1.25 mg (50,000 i.u.) then becomes necessary, and the vitamin must be injected into the muscle in order to bypass the intestine. When osteomalacia is related to kidney disorders even this dose is insufficient, and two or more times the amount may become necessary.

Osteoporosis (honey-combing of the bone) is the most common bone disease, and it particularly affects women past the menopause. It is due mainly to loss of bone calcium being faster than its replacement. Evidence has been presented by a team from Harvard Medical School, U.S.A. in *The New England Journal of Medicine* (1981) that one factor in the disease is a defective production of the hormone 1,25-dihydroxy vitamin D. This would explain why vitamin D itself is usually of little therapeutic use in osteoporosis but there is now hope that the active hormone 1,25-$(OH)_2$-D may be more beneficial.

Osteoporosis and the Menopause

Age-related osteoporosis occurs in both men and women with advancing age but women between the ages of 50 and 70 suffer more bone loss and related fractures than men. This increased incidence of osteoporosis in older women is believed to be related to hormonal changes occurring after the menopause. Hence, much attention has been focused on the protective effects of the sex hormone oestrogen.

One important factor influencing the chances of fracture is the quantity of bone mass present when the menopause approaches. The more that is present, the less the chances of developing osteoporosis. Thus, an adequate daily intake of calcium and vitamin D during the years leading up to the inevitable menopause may help the woman fend off the ensuing osteoporosis. Other factors that contribute to developing this bone condition are a reduction in intestinal absorption of calcium; a reduction in bone formation; an increase in bone loss of calcium and a decrease in the load-bearing capacity of the skeleton. The last factor is often brought about by continual bedrest or immobilization by plaster casts or by arthritis.

The relative importance of these various factors is disputed by various authorities. One recent review from King's College Hospital Medical School, London (*British Medical Journal* 1982) suggests that the primary cause of excessive bone loss in postmenopausal women is loss of ovarian function with the consequent decrease in oestrogen formation. It is lack of oestrogens that causes an increase in bone resorption, but the mechanism is not known. Other workers suggest that lack of excercise is important. A need for increased calcium requirements and lack of exposure to sunlight leading to vitamin D deficiency, have also been implicated. A leading article in *Lancet* (1982) recommends the most sensible approach to treating the condition, by taking into account the variety of contributory factors.

Once osteoporosis has been diagnosed, the aim of the treatment is two-fold. To prevent loss of bone mass (i.e. calcium phosphate) and to relieve the symptoms. The success of various treatments has been assessed by measuring bone mass and observing the fracture rate in those suffering from the complaint. The results, according to Drs J. C. Stevenson and M. I. Whitehead (*British Medical*

Journal 1982), favour oestrogen therapy as the best treatment to prevent bone loss and fractures. There is concern, however, that long-term oestrogen therapy may increase the risk of thrombosis and diseases of the uterus, including cancer.

Trials of calcium supplementation provide conflicting evidence of its effectiveness in preventing bone loss. The authors in the *BMJ* article conclude that though undoubtedly the diet should be adequate in minerals and vitamins, there is no convincing evidence that calcium supplements alone are an adequate treatment for postmenopausal bone loss. They consider, too, that vitamin D may show little benefit, but other studies have indicated that one defect in the osteoporotic patient is an inability to convert the inactive vitamin D to the highly active 1,25-dihydroxy vitamin D. Introduction of this more active metabolite into the general treatment of postmenopausal osteoporosis may thus be more promising.

Not everyone agrees with the assessment of Drs Stevenson and Whitehead, and other research workers (*British Medical Journal*, September and October 1982) claim that in their experience, calcium supplementation represents a valid alternative to oestrogen therapy. A *Lancet* (1982) review emphasizes the importance of monitoring calcium and vitamin D status and maintaining a calcium balance in osteoporotic postmenopausal women, particularly when the diet is poor and exposure to sunlight is minimal.

A recent trial, reported from the Mayo Clinic, U.S.A., and published in *The New England Journal of Medicine* (1982), provides guidance as to the treatment of osteoporosis. The researchers assessed the rates of spinal fracture in 165 patients with postmenopausal osteoporosis. Fifty-nine patients were treated with calcium (alone or with oestrogen) and/or vitamin D. Sixty-one were treated with sodium fluoride and calcium (again alone or combined with oestrogen) and/or vitamin D. Forty-five patients were left untreated to act as controls.

Fracture rates were reduced in all those treated with some form of therapy. Treatment with calcium alone or combined with oestrogen and/or vitamin D, reduced the overall fracture rate to half or less than that observed in untreated patients. The group receiving fluoride in addition to calcium had a 30 per cent lower fracture rate than those receiving calcium therapy. Those patients who received oestrogen therapy had a significantly lower fracture rate than those who did not. The most effective therapy was the combination of fluoride, calcium and oestrogen. Little additional benefit was shown by vitamin D, although this must have influenced the absorption of calcium from the supplements.

The authors of the study consider that the additive effect of fluoride and oestrogen was to be expected because of the potency of the former in stimulating bone formation and the latter in inhibiting bone loss. They question, though, whether the effectiveness of the oestrogen compensates for its possible adverse effects. They conclude that their study confirms the efficacy of combining available therapeutic agents with sodium fluoride in preventing the fractures associated with post-menopausal osteoporosis. Calcium supplementation is more efficacious in the presence of vitamin D so, whilst there may not be a direct effect of the vitamin in preventing this painful and disabling condition, it is essential to ensure maximum absorption of the minerals that are exerting a beneficial effect. A daily intake up to 1500 mg calcium and 400 i.u. vitamin D is the normal level of supplementation.

Vitamin D Status of Asians in Pakistan and the U.K.

We have seen that Asian immigrants in the U.K. are at risk of developing osteomalacia and rickets, although the actual numbers who develop these bone diseases is relatively small. Despite this, between 33 per cent and 44 per cent of Asian immigrants studied have biochemical evidence of vitamin D deficiency characterized by low blood concentration of 25-hydroxy vitamin D, the circulating form.

The specific reasons why Asian immigrants are more

prone to vitamin D deficiency, when compared with the
indigenous population of the U.K., are not known with
certainty. Various environmental and genetic factors
have been implicated, notably inadequate exposure to
the sun, dietary habits, skin colour and possibly even
some metabolic defect that reduces the efficiency of skin
production of the vitamin. A study of the vitamin D status
of Asians living in Pakistan compared to that of those
living in Rochdale was thus undertaken by a group of
medical researchers, and their results were published in
The British Medical Journal (1983).

In a previous study of 262 Asians living in Rochdale, 90
had originally come from the Lahore and Rawalpindi
areas of Pakistan. Enquiries in these areas led to the
discovery of 19 first degree relatives of those who emigrated
to Britain. The remaining 73 of the 92 people studied in
Pakistan were recruited from neighbours of those relatives.
They ranged in age from 11 to 75 years and were
considered to be representative of, and comparable to,
the Asians who had emigrated from that community. The
serum 25-hydroxyvitamin D levels of all participants
were measured. Clinical examinations were carried out to
ascertain any overt signs of vitamin D deficiency, and in
addition, a full dietary history was obtained for every
individual in order to assess dietary vitamin D intake.

The control group of 92 Asians living in Rochdale were
chosen such that their age and sex were identical to those
in the study group. Their ages ranged from 11 to 60 years.
Since 25-hydroxyvitamin D levels in the blood vary with
the seasons, this group had their blood measured in April
and a second group of controls, 62 in all, had their levels
determined in the Autumn. The results were quite en-
lightening.

None of the individuals living in Pakistan had clinical
signs of vitamin D deficiency. Their blood levels of 25-
hydroxyvitamin D were significantly higher than those in
their U.K. counterparts, both in the Spring and Autumn
groups. Women living in Pakistan had significantly lower
blood serum levels of 25-hydroxyvitamin D than the

men. There were no differences detected between city and village dwellers. However, calculated dietary intakes of vitamin D were lower, on average, in Pakistan than in Rochdale, despite the fact that the type of diet consumed was essentially the same in the two countries.

The higher serum 25-hydroxyvitamin D levels in those living in Pakistan indicates that their vitamin D status is generally excellent. It therefore looks as though adequate exposure to the sun by these people can maintain good blood levels of the vitamin, despite a small dietary intake. It is highly unlikely, on these figures, that Asians leaving Pakistan will enter the U.K. suffering from vitamin D deficiency. The findings thus confirm that the development of deficiency in immigrant Asians is the result of environmental change and not some inherent genetic trait of their race.

One clear conclusion to emerge from the study is that the principal source of vitamin D for Asians living in Pakistan is sunlight. There may, therefore, be several factors involved in producing lower blood serum levels of 25-hydroxyvitamin D in migrant Asians. One significant factor could be the reduced intensity of ultra violet light in Rochdale due to greater cloud cover, a more northerly latitude, and perhaps a polluted atmosphere. Coupled with this, the Asians' preference for a secluded lifestyle and the observance of *purdah* (screening of women as part of their religious practices) may contribute to their decreased skin production of vitamin D leading to low serum levels of 25-hydroxy vitamin D. This practice would explain the lower levels of the vitamin in the women of Pakistan compared to their men. Even so, the higher intensity of ultraviolet light in that country would appear to suffice to keep the blood levels of these women at a reasonable concentration. All other things being equal, the switch to a U.K. climate would, not surprisingly, produce lower blood serum levels of the vitamin.

The authors conclude that it is unlikely that education of the Asian community to increase their exposure to sunlight will be effective. There are moral objections to changing cultural practices that are related to religious beliefs. It is to be hoped that a switch to a western diet, with its increased intake of vitamin D, may serve to increase these people's vitamin status. Until these changes take place, however, the authors strongly recommend preventative measures against rickets and osteomalacia in the Asian community by the use of vitamin D supplements.

Rheumatoid Arthritis

As long ago as 1935, Drs I. Dreyer and C. I. Reed reported that clinical improvement of rheumatoid arthritis was observed with daily doses of 300,000 to 500,000 i.u. of vitamin D. Some confirmation was obtained from other researchers, but in 1938 Dr N. R. Abrams and W. Bauer, in *The Journal of the American Medical Association*, presented a controlled study that indicated no positive response from the vitamin in this condition. Interest then waned until the 1950's, when Dr O. Ahlborg of Scandinavia treated 500 sufferers of rheumatoid arthritis with 100,000 i.u. of vitamin D daily. He claimed marked clinical improvement with 70 per cent of those tested, which makes the therapeutic response with the vitamin comparable to potent drugs. Several months treatment was required before any benefit became apparent.

A controlled double-blind clinical trial (i.e. neither doctor nor patient knows whether they are giving or receiving treatment or an inactive placebo) of vitamin D was carried out in 1973 in Sweden. Twenty-four patients received 100,000 i.u. of the vitamin daily for a year; the remaining twenty-five patients received placebo. Improvements by both doctors and patients were observed in 67 per cent of the treated group and by 36 per cent of the control group. Deterioration of the condition occurred in the vitamin D-treated group only to the extent of 4 per cent but in the placebo-treated group the figure was 36 per cent. One pleasing factor for the vitamin D patients was a significant reduction in their consumption of painkillers and conventional drugs. After one year, these patients reported their morning stiffness had eased and their hand strength increased. No serious side-effects were observed.

The high intake of vitamin D required precludes self-treatment of rheumatoid arthritis with the vitamin, since such potencies are available on prescription only and must be taken under medical supervision. However, it does seem that prevention of the arthritic condition may be more likely with adequate body levels of vitamin D. These are best achieved with a good diet containing foods that are rich in vitamin D, plus adequate exposure to the sun to allow the skin to produce sufficient of the vitamin to supplement that in the food.

The Toxicity of Vitamin D

Vitamin D is the most toxic of all the vitamins when taken in excessive amounts. There is a narrow gap between its nutrient requirement and its toxic dose. As little as five times the recommended daily intake (50mcg or 2000 i.u.), taken daily over prolonged periods, has led to toxic symptoms in adults and in children. Unfortunately, some individuals are over-sensitive to excess vitamin D in the diet either because of hereditary reasons or because of disease. These people are more likely to develop toxic symptoms from slight overdose than their 'normal' counterparts.

The main problem induced by excessive vitamin D is the deposition of calcium in the soft tissues of the body such as the kidneys, the arteries, the heart and the lungs. This is because the control of maintaining blood calcium levels within normal limits is lost when too much vitamin D is present. Blood calcium levels rise as a result of over-absorption of the mineral from the food and its release from the bone at too great a rate. Hence, calcium starts to be deposited in areas where it would not normally be.

The mechanism is not excessive production of 1,25-dihydroxy-D, which we have seen is the most active hormonal form of the vitamin. What happens is that 25-hydroxy-D is produced in large quantities by the action of the liver on the ingested vitamin. This metabolite is not nearly as active as 1,25-dihydoxy-D on a weight-for-weight basis, but it is present in the blood in such high concentrations that it can cause the blood calcium to rise to alarming heights. The true toxic material is therefore 25-hydroxy-D.

Babies and young children are the most prone to suffer from vitamin D poisoning and some deaths have resulted. A typical case was reported in *Lancet* (1978). A nine-month old boy had been treated with drops containing vitamin D_2 from the age of six months. The reason was that his muscular movements were not developing normally. During the three months treatment he had received a massive total intake of 1,600,000 i.u. of the vitamin. As well as obvious symptoms (see below), X-rays showed calcium stones lodged in the kidneys. Treatment consisted of a diet devoid of calcium and vitamin D and eventually he improved and recovered when his blood calcium and 25-hydroxy-D levels returned to normal.

The usual reason for toxicity of vitamin D in an infant arises when the parent mistakes the recommended dose of a preparation, or gives some potent vitamin D preparation (usually called calciferol) by the teaspoonful in the mistaken belief that it is similar to cod liver oil, without realizing that it is some 50 times more potent. Sometimes toxicity arises because the child is given massive doses of the vitamin for the treatment of bone or kidney disease. Occasionally, a child may suffer toxic symptoms because circumstances dictate a massive dose at infrequent intervals (as in the third world). Whilst most of these children tolerate these vast intakes, occasionally some react, even though the benefits usually outweigh the disadvantages.

The early symptoms of overdose of vitamin D in a child include loss of appetite, nausea and vomiting. The child is constantly thirsty and passes large volumes of urine. Both diarrhoea and constipation may alternate. Often, bot not always, pains develop in the head that are different from conventional headaches. The child becomes thin, irritable and depressed, ultimately falling into a stupor. Eventually death results, and a constant finding at the post-mortem examination is massive deposition of calcium in the soft tissues and organs of the body. The only treatment for chronic overdose of vitamin D is to stop giving the vitamin and carefully controlling the calcium intake. Blood calcium levels must be constantly monitored, so treatment should be left to the medical practitioner.

Adults are not immune to poisoning themselves with vitamin D, albeit unwittingly. A report from a Manchester hospital, published in *Lancet* (1978), surveys six patients suffering from self-administered overdoses of vitamin D. Intakes varied from 50,000 i.u. daily for nine months to 100,000 i.u. daily for ten years. The shortest intake was 500,000 i.u. each day for only four months.

The symptoms were not unlike those encountered in vitamin D toxicity in children. Loss of appetite, weight loss, vomiting, signs of gastric ulceration and developing weakness were constant features. All exhibited the blood changes with too much calcium resulting in abnormal deposition within certain tissues. One woman even developed a growth of the shoulder-blade which eventually was found to be a conglomeration of calcium salts. All recovered when they were deprived of vitamin D and subjected to controlled calcium intake.

Even when under medical supervision, it is still possible for patients to become poisoned with vitamin D. A report from a Dundee hospital in *Lancet* (1980) surveyed 20 patients who were being treated with the vitamin for a variety of disorders. Intakes varied from 25,000 to 400,000 i.u. daily but most were taking 50,000 i.u. Since some patients were poisoned twice or three times there were 27 episodes of poisoning. In most of them the patients had loss of appetite, nausea or vomiting, weight-loss, headaches, and mental symptoms including apathy, fatigue and confusion. Twelve of them showed kidney function impairment that persisted in three patients even after treatment. There were two deaths amongst them, but these may have been caused by factors other than vitamin D overdose.

The reasons for taking too much vitamin D ranged from mistaken dosage to inadequate or infrequent monitoring of the patients' blood. Mistaken dosage usually related to confusion in the patients' mind between micrograms and milligrams – in one case the dose should have been 12.5 micrograms but 1.25 milligrams were actually taken – and ignorance of the high concentration of some standard dispensed medicines.

Vitamin D potency in preparations available for general sale are legally restricted in the UK to 400 i.u. (10 mcg) daily and it is sensible to observe strictly the suggested dose on these packs.

3.

K – THE BLOOD COAGULATION VITAMIN

In 1929, Henrik Dam, a medical student at the University of Frieberg, was investigating the biosynthesis of cholesterol in chicks. He prepared fat-free diets by extracting their feed with organic solvents. After about three weeks on this diet the chicks all acquired haemorrhagic disease. This is excessive bleeding due to an inability of the blood to form clots. Dam therefore concluded that some factor in the fat fraction of the diet was necessary to coagulate blood. The chick haemorrhagic disease was cured simply by giving a variety of foodstuffs amongst which lucerne (alfalfa) and putrified fish meal were the most effective. Dam named the factor vitamin K, an abbreviation for Koagulationsvitamin, a word derived from his native Danish.

The new vitamin was eventually isolated from lucerne and decayed fish meal by Dr Edward Daisy of St Louis University. It was then discovered by his group and by that of Dr Paul Karrer, a Swiss chemist, that the vitamin from the two sources showed structural differences. Thus, there were at least two different types of vitamin K, each biologically active. Soon the successful synthesis of both vitamins was announced from three different laboratories in the U.S.A. In 1943, Drs Dam and Daisy shared the Nobel Prize for their discoveries.

Types of Vitamin K

The vitamin K that exists in plants is known as vitamin K_1 and the names Phytomenadione, Phylloquinone and Phytylmenaquinone. There is only one vitamin K_1. On the other hand, the compound usually referred to as vitamin K_2, which was first isolated from putrified fish meal, is only one of a family of vitamins K. These are all produced by bacteria, and they differ from each other in the length of the carbon chains that are present in the basic structure of the vitamin. Hence, while the vitamin in plants, vitamin K_1, contains a 20-carbon chain, that produced by bacterial synthesis can contain between 20 and 65-carbon chains. They are usually abbreviated to MK-4 to MK-13 where the numbers refer to isoprenyl units, each unit containing 5 carbon atoms. As a group they are known as multiprenyl-menaquinones.

Despite the wide variation in carbon-chain length, all of these vitamins K are active within the body although vitamins K_2 have only 75 per cent of the biological activity of vitamin K_1. The synthetic type of vitamin K is much more simple in structural terms. It has no carbon chains, although the basic ring structure is identical to that in naturally-occurring vitamins. It is known as vitamin K_3 or menadione or menaphthone. Menadione has about twice the biological activity of the natural vitamins. A derivative of it called acetomenaphthone, also with vitamin K activity is of interest since it represents the only type of vitamin K available on general sale to the public in Great Britain.

Food Sources

The best food sources of vitamin K are fresh, green, leafy vegetables like broccoli, lettuce, cabbage, cauliflower, sprouts and spinach. As is usual for the fat-soluble vitamins, liver is also a good source but lean meat also supplies useful quantities. Despite the wide distribution in foodstuffs of vitamin K, it is difficult to assess a daily dietary intake since, as we shall see, bacterial synthesis in the large intestine is also a very important source of the vitamin. However, some information can be obtained from the vitamin K contents of foods and these are shown in Table 4.

Table 4

The Vitamin K Content of Foods

FOOD	VITAMIN K mg/100g
Broccoli	0.8
Lettuce	0.7
Cabbage	0.4
Spinach	0.6
String beans	0.29
Brussels sprouts	0.8
Cauliflower	3.6
Potatoes	0.08
Carrots	0.01
Tomatoes	0.03
Peas	0.4
Lean meat	0.1
Calf liver	0.15
Beef liver	0.2
Pig liver	0.6
Cow's milk	0.02
Human milk	0.002

Bacterial Synthesis of Vitamin K

The bacteria that normally inhabit parts of the large intestine have the ability to produce useful amounts of vitamin K in the form of K_2 and this can be absorbed and utilized by the body. The contributions of dietary and bacterial vitamin K are not known with certainty, but there is some indirect evidence that each source supplies about 50% of the requirements. This was the conclusion of Swiss researchers who reported their findings in the *International Z. Vitamin Forschung* in 1970. They analyzed the different types of vitamin K in the human liver. We

know that vitamin K_1 is obtained solely from the diet and
this was present to the extent of half the vitamin content.
The other half consisted of the K_2 family of vitamins that
come only by bacterial synthesis.

Daily Requirements of Vitamin K

Unlike all the other vitamins, there is no recognized daily
requirements of vitamin K. This is because no authority
can agree on the amount contributed by the diet and that
by bacterial synthesis. Since there is no evidence of
widespread deficiency, it is generally assumed that all are
replete in the vitamin except in those cases, discussed
later, where deficiency can be induced for various reasons.
However, attempts have been made to determine daily
requirements, usually by studying people who have been
proved to be deficient in the vitamin and then assessing
the amount of vitamin K needed to restore them to
normal.

Drs P. G. Frick, G. Reidler and H. Brogli studied four
such patients and reported their results in *The Journal of
Applied Physiology* (1967). Vitamin K deficiency is characterized by an inability of the blood to clot, so by giving the
vitamin they could determine how little was required to
allow normal blood coagulation times to be restored.
They achieved this with doses of 30 micrograms of
vitamin K_1 per kilogram body weight.

A different approach was adopted by Drs P. Barkhan
and M. J. Shearer who published their findings in *The
Proceedings of the Royal Society of Medicine* in 1977. They took
a patient who could not absorb the vitamin by oral routes
(and this of course includes both dietary and bacterial
sources) because of obstructive jaundice, and injected
vitamin K_1 directly into the blood stream. They concluded
that the adult daily requirement of vitamin K is about 40
micrograms per day.

The discrepancies in the conclusions of the two trials
are not apparent but may reflect differences in the way
the vitamin was given. Nevertheless, they indicate the
problems of determining daily dietary requirements of

vitamin K, that are exacerbated because of the meaningful contribution by bacterial synthesis in the large intestine. Little wonder that no official authority will commit themselves to a suggested minimum daily intake.

Losses During Cooking

Vitamin K is destroyed by acids, alkalis, oxidizing agents, light and ultra-violet irradiation. Since these factors rarely come into operation in domestic cooking methods, it is generally assumed that the vitamin survives during storage and in the kitchen. However, commercial processing may remove some of the vitamin K_1, and frozen foods tend to have lower values than the fresh variety, presumably because of treatment before processing.

The Metabolism of Vitamin K

Vitamin K is fat-soluble so, to be absorbed by the intestine, bile salts are needed. If bile flow is restricted because of gallstones, obstructive jaundice or liver disease, absorption of the vitamin is depressed considerably. Once it is absorbed it is rapidly carried to the liver, which is the only site at which it functions. Very little is stored in this organ; most of it is metabolized and excreted after performing its functions. Hence, in the absence of fresh amounts supplied from the diet and bacterial synthesis, depletion is rapid and deficiency symptoms can manifest themselves within a week.

The Function of Vitamin K

The only way in which vitamin K works in the body is in the control of blood coagulation. If vitamin K levels are very low, the time in which it takes blood to clot is prolonged to such an extent that even minor cuts in the skin can lead to extensive blood loss. Internally, lack of vitamin K can lead to spontaneous haemorrhage in the main blood vessels, causing life-threatening loss of blood.

The vitamin has no direct effect on the process of blood coagulation, but it is vital for the production of four specific proteins by the liver and it is these proteins that determine the coagulability of blood. These clotting factors are known as Prothrombin (Factor II); Proconvertin (Factor VII); Christmas factor (Factor IX) and Stuart-Prower factor (Factor X). As the amino acids are strung together to synthesize these four proteins, a stage is reached at which one of the amino acids, called glutamic acid, must be carboxylated for the proteins to perform their blood clotting function. Carboxylation cannot be introduced without the presence of vitamin K. Only then can these protein factors bind calcium, the mineral that is also necessary for the normal coagulation of blood. There is then a whole sequence of events involving all four factors, but the end result is the activation of the factor prothrombin to thrombin. Thrombin is a fibrous, insoluble protein that forms a web across the damaged blood vessel wall, and it is upon this base that red blood cells coagulate to form the plug we call a blood clot.

Deficiency of Vitamin K

Primary deficiency: For some time doctors and scientists have believed that a deficiency of vitamin K is impossible under normal circumstances, because of synthesis of the vitamin by intestinal bacteria. In fact, primary deficiency has been reported only once in medical literature (*Clinical Pathology*, 1977) in adults, but it can represent a problem in new born babies. Vitamin K deficiency is usually diagnosed, not by measuring the vitamin itself in the blood, but by assaying the quantity of prothrombin present. This is much simpler and, as we have seen, the amount of prothrombin present depends completely on the vitamin K available, so it gives an excellent indication of the vitamin's status.

Infants are particularly prone to vitamin K deficiency in the first few days of life because they have a sterile intestinal tract, so no bacteria are present to produce the vitamin. In addition, human breast milk is a very poor source of the vitamin although cow's milk can provide higher quantities. Studies reported in *Lancet* (1982) from Guys Hospital, London, indicate that transfer of vitamin

K across the placenta does not occur readily, so this factor also contributes to lack of the vitamin. Hence, the infant may be prone to the so-called haemorrhagic disease of the newborn, which is defined as a bleeding disorder in the first few days of life caused by a deficiency of vitamin K. The usual symptoms are bleeding from the stomach, the intestine, umbilical stump and operation sites on the second or third day after birth.

Treatment is simple, and involves giving 0.5 or 1.0 mg of vitamin K_1 with the first feed. Some paediatricians treat all newborn babies with the vitamin as a preventative measure, but the practice is by no means universally accepted. In only about one in 800 infants born does bleeding occur between the second and fifth days of life and it is felt in some obstetric units in Britain that this does not justify treating every newborn baby. It is comforting to know, however, that if haemorrhagic disease does develop the small amount of vitamin K needed to correct it is both effective and safe. It is only in the underdeveloped countries of the world that there may be a case for giving every baby a dose of vitamin K because haemorrhagic disease of the newborn is more prevalent. One reason for this may reside in the poor nutrition of the mother.

Induced deficiency: Any condition that gives rise to deficient absorption of fats may also reduce drastically the amount of vitamin K available to the body, since the vitamin is fat-soluble. Two such conditions are sprue and coeliac disease in which bleeding episodes related to vitamin K deficiency may occur. The secretion of bile salts is as necessary for absorption of the vitamin as for any other fats, and where the supply of these is curtailed, as in biliary obstruction, there is a greater chance of vitamin K deficiency. At one time, severe bleeding during, or a day or two after, an operation for the relief of jaundice due to biliary obstruction was a common occurrence much feared by surgeons. The introduction of vitamin K as a standard injection before operations has now reduced this danger considerably.

The commonest deficiency of vitamin K in adults is that induced by the prolonged administration of powerful antibiotics. The reason is that most antibiotics are not very selective and, whilst they are performing their job of killing harmful bacteria, they can at the same time reduce the 'friendly' bacterial population of the large intestine. These no longer produce vitamin K, and an important source of the vitamin is lost. When this is combined with a poor dietary intake of the vitamin, or with a condition of malabsorption of fats, the net result is a high tendency to bleed.

There are many studies confirming the dangers of prolonged antibiotic therapy on vitamin K status of the body. Typical is that of Dr G. F. Pineo of St Joseph's Hospital, Hamilton, Ontario, who studied 27 hospital patients over a period of 24 months. All patients were found to be deficient in vitamin K, due to a decreased food intake and treatment with antibiotics. This deficiency created problems of haemorrhage when these people underwent surgery. The researchers concluded that any unexpected serious bleeding during the early post operative period in those who have had antibiotics may be due to induced vitamin K deficiency. The remedy is simple, namely treatment with supplemental vitamin K, but the most important factor is to be aware of the detrimental effects of antibiotics on intestinal bacteria. In many hospitals, standard treatment for those on long-term antibiotics therapy is pure vitamin K, but this is not always the case for patients being treated outside hospital.

Low prothrombin levels in the blood are frequently encountered in patients with various liver disorders including viral hepatitis, cirrhosis and cancer. These cases rarely respond to vitamin K therapy, because the prime reason for low prothrombin (leading to increased chances of bleeding) is an inability of the diseased liver to make prothrombin. Once the organ starts to recover, however, its capacity for making prothrombin is restored, and blood clotting times revert to normal.

Anticoagulants

For many years it has been known that cattle fed on spoilt sweet clover develop a haemorrhagic disease, characterized by massive internal bleeding leading eventually to death. It was not until 1941, however, M. A. Stahmann, C. F. Huebner and K. P. Link of the University of Wisconsin, U.S.A., reported that they had isolated the factor responsible for the disease from the plant feed. The compound was named dicoumarol, and its discovery hailed a new era in treating thrombosis in man – a condition where the blood clots too readily. Most heart attacks and strokes are caused by blockage of major blood vessels with blood clots (or thrombi), so any compound that could reduce the tendency of the blood to clot was a major breakthrough.

Dicoumarol functions by neutralizing the effect of vitamin K, so it is known as a vitamin antagonist. Antagonists to many vitamins are known and they all share one common feature. Each is similar in structure to the vitamin they antagonize in such a way that they can attach themselves to the enzyme with which the vitamin is normally combined, so preventing the enzyme from carrying out its function. It is not unlike the lock and key principle. If the wrong key is put into a lock, it may be able to fit into it but the key will not turn. The keyhole is blocked so the correct key cannot be inserted and the door remains locked. Dicoumarol has a structure similar to, but is different in certain fundamental parts from, vitamin K. It therefore competes with the vitamin in the liver for the enzyme sites normally reserved for the vitamin and, when it wins, the enzyme is inactivated and no prothrombin is produced. The end result is similar to that when vitamin K is deficient, namely an increase in blood clotting time.

Dicoumarol has now been replaced by other, synthetic vitamin K antagonists, but they are all classed as anti-coagulants. One of the most widely used is warfarin, another compound that is similar in structure to vitamin K. Originally introduced as a rat poison, since its presence in bait induced massive haemorrhages in the rat when eaten, warfarin is used extensively in people who have suffered from thrombosis in the heart, brain, legs and other parts of the body.

It is possible, of course, that warfarin and other anti-coagulants work too well in neutralizing the action of vitamin K, and there is always the possibility that overdose of the anti-coagulant will induce bleeding. This is why patients who are on these drugs are constantly monitored for blood coagulability by measuring their prothrombin time. If an excess of anti-coagulant is taken, its effect can be neutralized by giving vitamin K. The balance between drug and vitamin K intakes is thus critical, which is why it must always be carried out under medical supervision.

Therapy with Vitamin K

The only therapeutic uses of vitamin K are in treating haemorrhagic disease of the newborn; in overcoming the inability to absorb the vitamin where this is due to disease of malabsorption or to lack of production of bile; in treating overdosage with anti-coagulant drugs; and some-times in overcoming the effects of long-term antibiotic therapy. None of these are suitable for self-treatment, apart perhaps from vitamin K deficiency induced by antibiotics. Anyone on this drug treatment should look to their diets and try to increase their intake of vitamin K-containing foods. This is perfectly safe, and there is no record yet of anyone suffering from thrombosis because of an excessive intake of the vitamin in their diet.

Unfortunately, vitamin K has no place in treating the hereditary disease of haemophilia which is characterized by an inability of the blood to clot. In this disease, some of the other factors concerned with blood coagulation appear to be defective but none of them are related to vitamin K.

INDEX